Investing in Real Estate: from 0 to the million

Based on my personal story - how I became
a successful real estate investor

Adapted to be country-independent
(and to include examples in North America and Europe)

Artur Mariano, PhD

About the author

Artur Mariano, PhD, Artur Mariano, PhD is a computer science engineer, and graduated MSc from University of Minho (Portugal) – with a period at the University of Texas at Austin – and holds a PhD on post-quantum cryptography (applied math) obtained from the Darmstadt University of Technology (Germany). He published dozens of scientific papers, some of which were published on tier 1 conferences on cryptography, post-quantum computing, parallel computing or applied math.

He is a Real Estate investor for more than a decade now, and holds a portfolio of dozens of units through his holding. He co-founded ArrowPlus (**www.arrowplus.pt**), a company that helps investors to find below-market real estate deals, with large yield potential. He also invests, through ArrowPlus, in small businesses and startups in different sectors.

He spends a great deal of his time doing research, but he also writes regularly about business models, investing and real estate. As a real estate consultant, serving several clients and companies, he acquired considerable experience in the industry, which he now makes available through this book. Currently, he is also an analyst at Empiricus Research Portugal, through ArrowPlus, writing about real estate investing.

LEGAL DISCLAIMER: Although this book is about real estate investing, it doesn't offer any kind of guarantees. To invest, always consult with a licensed advisor.

Even when the author suggests that he obtained certain results, it does not mean that the reader will obtain the same results, because the experience, knowledge and action of each person are different. The publisher and the author of this book cannot be held accountable for any loss or trauma caused to the readers, directly or indirectly due to the content of this book.

While writing this book, all efforts were made to ensure that the book is free of mistakes and errors. However, the publisher and the author will we not be liable for any loss, trauma or damage, including consequential damages, if any, caused by a reader's use of any information in this book, even if the information in this book is faulty, incorrect or incomplete. This book was written based on the experience of his author and reflects his opinion on the subject.

Be careful with your money. Only use strategies you fully understand and whose risks you fully understand and are comfortable taking. You should NEVER rely upon any information contained in this book to invest or act.

Furthermore, this book does not intend, in any way or format, to qualify, judge or make vulnerable any entity or person. The content of this book is simply the result of the knowledge and experience of its author.

Finally, this book does not provide any kind of advice pertaining to investment, taxes or any other subject. Do not take any of the content of this book as investment, financial, tax or any other type of advice, because it is not. Invest at your own risk.

Although the author and publisher have made every effort to ensure that the information in this book was correct at press time, the author and publisher do not assume and hereby disclaim any liability to any party for any loss, damage, or disruption caused by errors or omissions, whether such errors or omissions result from negligence, accident, or any other cause.

Preface

Time has shown that real estate is one of the best vehicles to create wealth, when used properly and is done based on sound knowledge. Sadly, in many countries such as my own – Portugal - there is a lack of a mature culture in real estate investing, I believe, this is due to the lack of materials and resources that provide the necessary knowledge to allow any person to invest in real estate.

This book, in my opinion, addresses that gap. Inspired by the knowledge I acquired in real estate investing over time, after more than 10 years investing in real estate (either directly or indirectly), I believe I came up with a fantastic work that will help any investor: from the beginner investor who wants to start off but does not know how, to the experienced investor, who can benefit a lot from my own experience, models and tools, which I provide in this book.

This book is intended to help investors improve their knowledge about real estate, and I adapted it to be generic in terms of markets and countries. Literally from 0 to the million, I introduce several tools that include methods to find investment properties, relationship with the main players in the industry, such as banks, agents and tenants, and ways to structure a portfolio so that it becomes a million-dollar portfolio.

Be prudent, careful or daring in your investments – whatever you feel that suits your profile the best. But do it always based on sound knowledge.

INDEX

	Preface	v
1	Foundations of real estate investing	3
2	See yourself as an investor	16
3	Strategies, models and goals	23
4	Financing	33
5	Other financial aspects	47
6	Negotiating with lenders	56
7	Searching and negotiating properties	69
8	Renovation works	83
9	Rent out/sell your real estate	91
10	Scale your portfolio until the million	101
11	Keep yourself at the top	114
12	After this book	123

Artur Mariano

1

Foundations of real estate investing

I start this book from the beginning: the foundations of real estate investing. It is possible that the author knows various entrepreneurs or business owners who have no formal education on management or business that, despite that, are successful. In a global scale, we can even find many examples of people who have succeeded brilliantly even without this kind of education. There is, therefore, sufficient evidence that this – being very successful without education - is perfectly possible.

However, the truth is that education on a specific area does help tremendously with the execution of a business, project or investment. I mean, we can indeed find several examples of people who were not highly educated and still became successful. There is sufficient evidence that this is totally possible.

However, the truth is that advanced training in a given area can only help (in most cases tremendously) in the execution of a business, project or investment. I mean, it is probable to find people who became successful without ever going to college, but my point is that even those people would in theory benefit from training.

This is why I consider this chapter of high importance, both to beginners and experienced real estate investors. Moreover, I will use terms throughout this book which I would like the reader to be familiar from this point on. Please notice that I may define some of these terms in differently than other authors.

If you feel you do not need to read this chapter, you may skip it and come back to it if need be.

Terms of real estate investing

If you already read other books on real estate investing, you will realize that many books start with definitions of terms that pertain to real estate investing. The main reason to do this is because, unlike other types of investment, there is considerable divergence in the semantics of these terms. Real estate is governed by specific rules and norms that change considerably (and recurrently) from country to country. As I have multiple years of experience in real estate investing, while also having dealt with clients from several countries, I can tell you that investors from different countries tend to think of real estate investing in very different ways. After all, each country has its own rules, when it comes to real estate.

In this chapter, the reader will find my own definitions of several terms that pertain to real estate investing, which I have been using for years. These will be vital in order to understand the remaining chapters of this book, especially the technical details and formulas I will present. Please keep in mind that some definitions I will introduce may be different from the definitions of other authors. Also, these may also collide with some fiscal terms.

Cash flow

"Cash flow" is the total amount of money that a given property generates. This term has several variants and several authors define cash flow differently. Usually, I use the terms "gross cash flow" and "net cash flow". The gross cash flow is the total income of a given rental property before any expenses, including property taxes and financial expenses (for instance, mortgage installments). The net cash flow takes into account all the expenses incurred in order to ultimately generate the rental income.

Like I said, there are more variations of the term "cash flow", however all of the terms and concepts I present in this book are based on "gross cash flow" and "net cash flow", and thus you only need to keep these two terms in mind in order to understand the examples I present throughout this book.

Operating expenses

The operating expenses are all the expenses necessary for the property to generate rental income. These include, among others, insurance, maintenance, property taxes and others.

Note that, within these expenses, I do not include financial expenses, such as interest on mortgages or taxes on the rental income (cash flow).

Yield

The yield on any real estate deal is the cash flow over the total amount invested, i.e. yield = *cash flow* / total investment.

If we talk about gross yield, that means that we consider the gross cash flow in the formula, which means that the yield does not take taxes or expenses into account.

If we talk about net yield, then we deduct all the expenses with the property to the formula, which is the same as using the net cash flow.

In a real estate deal, as I will show you later in this book, it is necessary to assess the quality of the yield as well. However, the quality of the yield is not analytical (and not a term per se), therefore I talk about this problem later in the book.

Vacancies

Vacancies are usually show as a percentage, based on the time that a given property was not rented out during the year. Therefore, they indicate the percentage of time that the property (asset) did not generate income (cash flow), due to being vacant.

Payback

The payback of a given real estate deal is the time, in years, that runs until the real estate investor gets his total investment back.

Note, however, that as with other terms, this should only be estimated at the beginning or end of a given real estate deal. This is because there is a number of variables that are not known at the beginning of the investment, such as the maintenance of the property, vacancies, etc.

Cash on cash return

The payback of an investment is an important metric, but there is another metric that is equality or even more important to assess on a given real estate deal: the cash on cash return. This is measured as a percentage of capital that is paid back, in a given year, regarding the total investment. This term is usually more applicable for investments where there is a reduced percentage of the investor's own money (meaning that there is leverage).

Consider the following example. The investor acquires a property that costs $100.000, but as he was able to finance 80% of the operation, he only had to put down $20.000. On top of the $20.000, he also had to pay $10.000 in taxes, commissions and other expenses. Therefore, he got into the deal with $30.000. Let us assume the net cash flow of that investment is $6.000, in the first year. That means that the cash on cash return will be 20%. It is more common to use the net cash flow when calculating the cash on cash return, although the gross cash flow can also be used.

Appreciation

Appreciation represents the value gained by real estate in a given period, usually in an automatic way. For example, if a given property is worth $100.000 and its value increases to $120.000, then we can say the property appreciated $20.000 or 20%.

LTV (Loan to value)

The LTV ("*Loan-to-Value*") is the percentage of a loan that is provided, for a given property value. It basically expresses the ration of a loan to the value of a given asset. For instance, if a given property is worth $100.000 and a bank loans an investor $70.000, then the LTV of the operation is 70%. The other 30% is commonly referred to as "the bank's haircut".

Although in the US it is common to calculate the LTV based on the property worth, in some countries in Europe it is common to apply the LTV to the maximum between the acquisition and the appraisal.

Other terms

In this section, I wanted to give you an overview of the most used terms in real estate investing, and, more than that, give you my own definitions so that you can entirely understand my message throughout this book (because, like I said, it is common to see divergent definitions across real estate investing books).

However, there are more terms that I would like to introduce. The first term is "REIT", which is the abbreviation for "Real Estate Investment Trusts". These are companies that invest in real estate with money from investors. There are REITs that operate in a given country, continent or even the entire world. Most REITs focus on a specific type of real estate (such as healthcare, retail, etc) and can both own real estate to rent out or buy and sell real estate. Note that, for any company to qualify as a REIT, it must meet certain guidelines. REITs usually trade on stock exchanges and therefore provide investors with the possibility to invest in real estate through a liquid stake.

Real estate vs other investments

In my opinion, there is only a handful of possible investments. Beyond real estate, we can essentially invest in businesses (either through the stock market or with our own business), bonds and loans. The majority of the other investments you can find are typically derivatives and/or combinations of these. Starting our own business is not a passive investment, but a rather active one. I will focus on passive investments, because those are more comparable with real estate than those that are active.

Real estate has a number of advantages compared to other investments, but I won't lie to you: depending on your investor profile, real estate may not necessarily be the best investment for you. In the following, I will show you the advantages and disadvantages, from a generic standpoint, of real estate investing. You should think, based on your investment profile, whether this is indeed the best path for you to follow. I believe that real estate investing is the best way to accumulate wealth, due to different factors, but not all investors are tailored to invest in real estate.

Next, I will show you several advantages that real estate investing has over other investments.

Real estate is a natural investment

A lot of us are exposed to real estate since new. For most of us, our parents use to worry about paying the rent or the mortgage. Some of us are lucky enough to come from a household where we heard about "renegotiating the interest rate". Some of us had no choice but hearing "the rent is due and I do not know how I will pay for it". Either way, most of us come from a background where real estate was present all along.

But this is not the case for other investments, such as the stock market. In Portugal, where I come from, people even say "play" in the stock market. In most European countries the stock market is not regarded as a safe investment; in fact it is quite the opposite – it is regarded as an unsafe way to park money, or even play with it. But in no country people say "play" with real estate, I am certain.

In many European countries people regard the stock market as a speculation marketplace, that carries considerable risk, and therefore only a few take the plunge. Real Estate, on the other hand, is regarded as safe. For instance, in my country people think that real estate is so safe that homeownership rates are sky high.

Buying assets below market value

Imagine you see a property listed for $100.000 and somehow you end up convincing the owner to sell it to you for a lower figure, say $80.000. You can use negotiation techniques (which I also cover in this book), good arguments, your own skills of convincing people, etc.

You may ask yourself "why on earth would someone sell me a property $20.000 below market value"?

Well, there are many possible reasons for that. For instance, imagine the seller needs that money to close another deal, which he believes is way too good to pass on. Let's even be practical: imagine that the seller can actually buy another property worth $130.000 for only $80.000 (he already has another buyer who would buy the property from it for $110.000). The catch is, he needs to close on this property right away, and so he needs the money. But who would not lose $20.000 on one deal, if there was another deal where one could make $30.000 ($110.000 - $80.000)?

This is of course a very specific reason and of course it is not what happens 100% of the time. But the truth is that I see properties sold below market value every single day…

Now imagine the same situation for other investment vehicles. In the stock market, for instance, you can find and buy stocks for a good price, with regards to what the company is actually worth, but you cannot buy them below market value. By definition, what you pay for them is actually their market value.

Real Estate is tangible

Stocks, among other investments, are not objects you can touch. As for real estate, on the other hand, you can see it and touch it. This argument has, most of the time, an emotional side attached: many investors feel comfortable seeing and touching their assets. It is part of the human nature, because it is connected to the sense of ownership. At the same time, if real estate collapses or implodes, in principle the investor will be safe as there is insurance to cover that risk. But for real estate, the truth is that companies may file for bankruptcy and collapse, leaving shareholders with nothing in their hands.

It is easier to leverage in real estate

Using Other People's Money (OPM), asking for a loan, leveraging. Different terms for the same thing. But this is way easier with real estate than other types of investment. For instance, have you ever imagined what it would be like to go to a bank and ask for a loan to invest in the stock market? I am not saying you cannot get a loan to that end, but we are certainly talking about a type of loan that is harder to obtain and has higher interest rates that common real estate mortgages.

It is easier to create value with real estate

How could we create value buying stocks? There are very little ways of doing that – the only one I can think of right now is to buy stocks and sell them below market value on purpose.

With real estate, that is totally different. One of the reasons I prefer real estate over any other type of investment is because real estate allows one to set up a business – with all that comes with it. For example, if an investor buys enough properties to make $50.000 per year in rental income, we could compare that small real estate business to any business.

As I am about to tell you, a successful business is set up under the premise that it creates more value than not-so-successful businesses. Now let us talk about creating value with real estate. The entrepreneur (I am not calling him investor anymore) buys properties and rents them out for less than the market value, or remodels them so that they end up way nicer than the standard property in the neighborhood. How could you do this with stocks?

Real Estate has a purpose: being our homes

Real estate, unlike other investments, serve a purpose of being a home. For that reason, they will always be necessary (unless someone creates an alternative to houses – which will be difficult, at least in the next 3 generations or so).

On top of that, as population continues to grow, real estate will benefit from a positive ratio between the offer and the demand (the universal law that governs any market) also because land is way more limited than population growth potential.

Real Estate values are less volatile

Real estate has lower volatility given that properties do not have (yet, at least) real time quotes – in a very unscientific way, we can say that this contributes to lower the incidence of heart disease…

This does not mean that, occasionally, there are no big price oscillations, because they may exist. I have personally seen real estate being sold with 50% (if not more) profit margins solely because the market value had increased a lot in that (very small) period.

However, this tends to be the exception, not the rule. Especially when compared to stocks, where volatility is way more frequent and abrupt. In other words, in real estate, the perception of prices is way more spread over time and therefore slower than in the stock market. But I am not telling you that volatility is necessarily bad, because you can make a lot of money buying and selling assets (which is usually what "traders" do). However, these investors will always be, percentage-wise, smaller than regular investors, because among other reasons trading requires a lot of time and almost becomes a full-time job per se.

Real Estate has many tax advantages

This book does not intend to cover taxes extensively, and you should always look for a licensed accountant to know more about taxes. However, based on my experience, real estate is so awesome from a tax standpoint that I cannot avoid this subject.

Real estate allows you, among many other things: 1) not to pay taxes on gains with properties if you reinvest the capital, under certain circumstances, 2) not to have any capital gains before the tax authority while you in fact capital gains (economical vs financial), and 3) write off many expenses against your (rental) income, to mention a few.

Real estate is an hedge against inflation

Unlike other investment vehicles, real estate is directly protected against inflation, or, in other words, it is an hedge against it.

Give the following problem a thought. Economy is growing too fast, in a given period, and inflation rises tremendously. If you have assets which do not keep up with inflation (a deposit on a savings account), in fact you may actually end up poorer (if we consider purchasing power as wealth), even if that asset brought you some income. For instance, imagine that inflation is 5% and the savings account has a 2% interest rate on it. At the end of the year, on a $100.000 deposit, you will make $2.000 and therefore end up with $102.000 in the bank. However, to keep the same purchasing power, you should have $105.000 in your account, so you actually became poorer.

If inflation is high, it is usually reflected on rentals. Every time you rent out a property, rents should keep up with inflation and so you are automatically protected against it. If you do long-term leasing contracts, make sure to have this into account, by accounting for automatic increases in rent.

2

See yourself as an investor

Have you ever thought that nobody taught you anything about money at school? But is that correct, if money is one of the most important things in our lives? After all, we work 8 hours every day to make money. We cannot live without money in the current society we have, that is a fact; whether we want it or not, money has an undeniable importance in the current model of society we live in, and therefore in our lives.

For example, many of us have problems due to money. Do you know any couple who broke up due to money? Or any couple who, at least, discusses a lot due to money? Do you perhaps know someone who is never happy and suffers because of his/her financial situation?

The truth is that money is present in our lives and we cannot go around it, regardless how we decide to regard it.

Saving and investing – for taking us to a better financial situation – are two universal laws. The problem is that only a few people have the financial literacy that is necessary to make good financial decisions, such as saving and investing. And there are a lot of people who, with some extra education, could have a totally different lifestyle – with a lot less problems. If they could only manage money…

To invest, you need to see yourself as an investor. Whether you want to be a big or small investor, take it seriously. You never heard that what deserves to be done, deserves to be nailed? I have had clients of several types and profiles. Small investors, who looked for real estate to avoid banks. I have had other clients – small and big – who were pure capitalists. I myself love business and the concept of it. I like to study business models, even if I don't apply them. I also believe in a business model that creates a lot of value for clients (that is why I wrote a section called "being a real estate entrepreneur"). And I believe that the universe is an abundant place, where everyone can win.

When I thought out this book, I realized it would be better to make it a mostly-technical book. This chapter is an exception to that. It is true that it has a technical foundation – it is necessary to take investing seriously to nail it, like a true investor, whatever your relationship with money and life philosophy is. However, this chapter intends to break one of the biggest barriers there is when someone starts investing, or needs to access a new level: his/her relationship with money.

The meaning of money

My impression is that, in the society where I grew up in – the Portuguese one – a lot of people believe money is bad. This is also true in other societies where I lived in, although to a much smaller extent. I spent a lot of time in the US and Germany. I traveled the entire world. All in all, most people regard money the same way.

Have you ever seen someone commenting, with a critical tone, that another person was "too" ambitious? Have you ever perhaps heard expressions like "(s)he is all about money" or "money is not everything in life" after someone became successful, financially-wise? Sometimes it is envy. Sometimes it is frustration. Sometimes it is just this bad meaning that people attribute to money.

When I walked into a bank to ask for my first loan to buy a house, I explained the banker my well-though plan. My idea was to build a big real estate portfolio, based on my method that allows me to find properties well below their market value. Her response was unbelievable: "but why on earth would you like to have so many houses? Money is not everything in life… I myself only want the money I really need.". Yes, I am talking about the banker who was trying to sell me a mortgage loan. Unbelievable, right?

This is probably the least-technical opinion I write on this book, but I will say it anyway: in my opinion, the majority of people who criticize others ambition make it due to envy. Envy is a big problem in modern world. Especially in a world where we almost have to be ambitious in order to succeed. I am not saying that there is no one who genuinely believe that investing is not necessary, building wealth is bad, etc. I simply think that this is more the exception than the rule.

In the country I grew up in, Portugal, money and capitalism are still somewhat taboos. More often than not, when someone comes through as ambitious, that regarded as something bad. You must build a genuine relationship with money, which is part of this chapter's goal. Money should mean something important to you. It may be financial independence, helping family out or simply being happy building wealth. Whatever it is for you, be genuine about it. Do not let other opinions and criticism to change that and always be true to yourself.

Always remember that, as with everything, we can use things for the good or for the bad. A knife can be used to spread butter on bread, shaping a wood masterpiece or kill someone. A screwdriver can be used to repair a pipe or puncture a tire. Money by itself does not mean anything. What you do with is what truly counts. And I believe that most people do not understand one thing about wealth: it allows one to create value for others.

The essence of investing

You should have a strong reason to start investing. Whatever it is, have that reason in mind when investing. In my own case, there was an essential reason why I wanted to invest: I had the vision of becoming financially independent and leverage on that to create more value. Today I have a different vision: impact the largest possible number of people.

Your reasons may not have anything to do with mine, or the reasons of others. And it does not really matter; it just have to be genuine and foster you to make everything you can so that that vision comes true. As I said before, money per se does not mean anything good or bad. Define your genuine reason for investing and do not let yourself be influenced by anyone.

Vision

What separated Mark Zuckerberg in 2004 from any other young entrepreneur of the same age, with as much or even more talent than him? Why has Zuckerberg founded one of the biggest companies in the world, that impacts more than 2 billion lives today, and so many other entrepreneurs did not even manage to keep their companies afloat for more than 12 months?

There is a series of reasons why this happened, but I would like to point out one: vision. Have you ever heard the saying "businesses do not fail, only entrepreneurs do"?. Many studies show that the main reason why so many startups fail within 12 months or less is due to lack of vision from the entrepreneur who founded the company.

Vision is absolutely necessary in any sector, but in an investment or a business, it is especially relevant, in my opinion. So, have one. Create it. See it. Experiment it before you achieve it. And focus on it while investing. Have it on your sight and do everything you can to make it a reality. As long as you have a genuine motivation and you are willing to do what needs to be done, you will succeed.

The only rule is believe that no vision is either too big is only available to other people. Ray Kroc escalated McDonalds from a single dependency in San Bernardino to one of the biggest companies in the world after he was 50. Zuckerberg founded a company that impacts more than 2 billion lives, all from his bedroom. Elon Musk created a reusable rocket for the first time. Before these people did it, it seemed impossible, right?

I created several visions throughout my life, and they were the reason why I could achieve financial independence and have a PhD before turning 30. How about you, what goals do you have, where do you want to be in the future and why? Create your own vision and fight for it!

Lastly, I would like to challenge you to create your own future. If you do not create your future, somebody will, someone said. Your vision should allow you to see a bright future and, above all, a future you want to have. Life is too short to live a life we do not want to live. And too short to leave for tomorrow what we can do today. And since we only have one, it is just foolish not to live it to its full potential.

Be a real estate entrepreneur

There is a clear difference between entrepreneurship and investment. An entrepreneur can succeed even without knowing how to invest (and vice versa). But in my opinion, these are two vectors that eventually overlap with each other.

I believe that it is possible to be an entrepreneur in real estate. I do not think this is the right path to every investor, though. I think that only a small percentage of investors should be real estate entrepreneurs. Why entrepreneurs? Because they implement a business model, base their entire strategy on creating value for others and think about their real estate portfolio just like any other business. I call this a "real estate business" instead of "real estate investing".

Some of the features of a real estate business include the creation and maintenance of a business structure. It should support several business angles, including customer support, financing, accountancy, marketing and... creation of value. Creating value is, in my opinion, especially important. That is ultimately what differentiates a business from an investment.

Produts, prices... value!

How to create value in real estate? Creating value is something complex, dubious to assess and most of the time only considered by the best entrepreneurs.

For example, a given retail business sells a product; buys it for X and sells it for Y. Does it create any value? Yes it does. After all, customers could not have access to a similar business, or have to travel long distances to obtain the same products. There is value for the end client. How about SpaceX, which created a reusable rocket for the first time, while lowering the cost of rockets altogether? If we take into account the impact of these companies in terms of number of lives they impact, we will certainly conclude that the second company creates higher value.

I will give you my definition of creating value: lowering the cost of a product, to the largest number of people possible, while maintaining the quality of the competitor products. Another alternative is to keep the same price of competition, but raise the quality of the products significantly. Or better yet, but something that only the best entrepreneurs are capable of, is raising the quality of the product while lowering the price altogether.

In real estate, this means selling or renting real estate, whose "quality" is above average and "cost" is below average. For instance, I always break a sweat so that my real estate looks prettier, more functional and provide more comfort than the other ones on the market, for a given segment of properties. On top of that, I make sure my rents are below market value. I am a buy and hold investor, but the same logic can be applied to fix and flip.

Do, dominate, care

To this day, I have met and dealt with several real estate investors. Many are friends, others are partners, most were clients from my consulting company. As such, I have been exposed to many investing profiles. And there is a type of profile that find remarkable: the investor who is also a philanthropist, the investor who wants to do more for people. In this regard, there was a particular investor who I recall to this day. He had a very ambitious plan, but what caught my attention was his desire to provide for others. His plan was to build a portfolio what was so large he could create jobs for everyone in his community, which had been severely affected with the shutdown of a factory where most people worked at.

He came to my company so he could scale his already decent sized portfolio. I commended him for his vision, which like I said before is absolutely essential to succeed in any kind of investment. First, one has to do, then we need to dominate and only then we can care. We can care with the goal of our investment, helping the community, charity, etc. What I want to tell you is that there is a natural order for everything. Think about creating value, be an entrepreneur if that is what you want. But have a vision since day 1. Do not let your final goal to interfere with your journey – believe me, you will do more for others once you succeed yourself.

3

Strategies, models and goals

I have got several references and role models in my life. As I have been a scientist for a long time, my biggest reference is Percy Julian, who although not famous, was one of the greatest scientists of the last century.

In business, I always followed Warrant Buffer, although my role model is Elon Musk, founder and CEO of Tesla. As I love to learn about business models, I follow several entrepreneurs and TV shows about entrepreneurship, such as "Shark Tank". But why am I telling you this? Let us take my ultimate reference in business, Elon Musk. If you know Tesla, you know it is a company that does something very special and different: it makes products that are in fact revolutionary in the world, with a design that almost everyone loves, while being simultaneously more efficient (and cheaper, if we consider their segment) than its competitors. Tesla cars are cheaper than the equivalent cars from other brands, faster and safer (Tesla's Model S achieved the highest safety rate among all cars tested to this day).

After studying entrepreneurs for years, as well as business models, companies and people who succeed, I need to tell you a very important thing: only those with a clear strategy, a goal and (most often than not) a solid vision actually manage to pull it off. Regardless we talk about science, business or any other sector, well succeed people (whatever definition of success you want to use) always have a strategy. And that is what you should have, before anything else, in order to be successful in real estate investing.

In this chapter, I will briefly introduce you some strategies and popular models to invest in real estate. At the same time, I will explain you why goals (especially to those who want to invest thought their lives) are so necessary.

Investment strategies

In the last chapter, I talked about vision, which is really the driving force of any investor and entrepreneur. Now, I talk about strategies, which are the algorithm that makes us turn a vision into reality.

In our lives, we use strategies often. The human brain is always coming up with short-term strategies to make our lives easier. Otherwise, we would not think about alternative ways to get to a place faster, when we are in a hurry. We would not be able to improvise or think out of the box.

The use of strategies, however, is way broader than this. For instance, to write this book, I came up with a strategy: first I thought about the chapters, then the sections and subsections and before actually start writing I left bullet points with ideas I wanted to write about, throughout the book.

In real estate, this is no different: the use of strategies is crucial to our success in real estate investing. The investor should use strategies to start investing, find deals, finance transactions, negotiate with sellers and banks, and achieve the vision that made him/her start in the first place.

I will now show you the most known strategies and techniques in real estate investing, according to my personal perspective. I will not suggest you any specific strategy, because each investor should choose his/her path based on his/her own investor profile and goals, as I tell you later on this in this book.

Buy and hold

The first strategy to invest in real estate is to create a "buy and hold" portfolio, which essentially means that the investor buys properties and rents them out. This is the most common strategy in long-term real estate investing, and it is also what I have been following ever since I started. This strategy is tightly connected to getting the highest possible yields, and it is also used by most REITs, which buy properties, rent them out and distribute the profits among the investors in the REIT.

This strategy can be thought of as a way to "buy a salary", i.e., creating passive rental income that can be used as a salary/cover living expenses. This is one of the most common goals among the new clients of my company (my company identifies real estate properties below market value), right after those who want to put their savings to work. I have also worked with companies that intended to put their capital reserves to work, sometimes as a way to help to cover or even cover completely the operational costs of the company.

The "buy and hold" strategy has many different models, which I present later on.

Fix and flip

The second strategy, on the other side of the spectrum, is the "fix and flip" strategy. This is based on buying houses that can be resold, most often than not after being renovated and in the shortest timespan possible. Usually, those who follow this strategy buys another house after selling the previous one, as soon as he/she closes a transaction. Note that, in general, this strategy is more risky than "buy and hold", although that depends specifically on the investments, markets chosen, among other variables. Either way, this strategy requires, in general, more capital than buy and hold, because 1) remodeling houses can often be more expensive than actually predicted, 2) requires buying more than one house simultaneously (otherwise it is necessary to wait for every transaction in order to do another flip).

There are different models that can be followed under this strategy, which I show and comment on later on in this chapter.

Financing

Financing is extremely important in real estate investing, and therefore I dedicated an entire chapter for it (Chapter 4). However, I must say outright that the investment strategy that you pick will influence the financing strategy you should follow. In general, banks require two different indicators (which increases chances of financing) to lend money. The first one is a guarantee, when the loan is given, that is worth at least the same amount of the loan (for a given LTV; i.e. for a e.g. 80% LTV, the bank will loan the investor $100.000 if the property is worth $125.000).

The second indicator is the financial executability of the operation. That is, a financial plan that covers the mortgage payments. If we are talking about a primary property, then banks will probably look at the buyer's income and analyze whether, in principle, the buyer will afford to pay the mortgage without defaulting. Of course that the investor may default regardless of how high and stable his income is, but the higher the income, the smaller the probability of default. Plus, the bank will retain the mortgage so that there is a real asset in case of a default.

Buy and hold investment models

We can look to models as a generalization of one or more strategies. That means, a model includes one or more strategies and describes how those strategies are applied and executed, towards a specific goal. Models must be defined based on personal and conjectural facts, as I show you later on. Usually, models are only applied in buy and hold strategies, because these are usually applied long-term (vs fix and flip, which are usually planned for the short-term).

This is a description of an investment model: "I will only acquire high-yield properties and use rental income to remodel other properties I already have or buy more properties". More than a strategy, you are determining how to proceed to apply the strategy over time. This is in fact the description of a well-known model – cash flow maximization – as I will show you above.

Now, I will describe two different investment models for buy and hold strategies, which have been previously presented by other people. These two models are on both ends of the spectrum. Although it is impossible to describe every single model possibility, you can imagine any model between these two models as possible.

Free cash flow/cash flow maximization model

The first model is a model where the investor focuses on, above anything else, on the monthly cash flow of each investment he makes. For instance, if we were to choose between two properties that cost $100.000 (let's assume equal mortgage payments), the investor would choose that with the highest net cash flow. If property 1 puts $200/mo in your pocket and property 2 puts $300/mo in your pocket (both after mortgage payments and taxes), then property 2 is more suited for this model, even if we expect property 1 to appreciate more over time.

This model premise is that the investor either needs the surplus of his/her investments, or can invest that surplus at a higher rate than the appreciation rate of other properties (in this case property 1).

Let us assume that, for the example I have presented above, the investor expects property 1 to appreciate 4% every year and property 2 to appreciate at 2% a year. This means that, over a 10-year timespan, property 1 will appreciate $40.000 (10 years * 4% * $100.000 initial worth) and a total of $24.000 ($200 * 12 months * 10 years) in net rental income. Property 1 will then return $64.000 ($40.000 + $24.000), over a 10 year period.

Property	Appreciation (10 years)	Net rental income (10 years)
1	$40.000	$24.000
2	$20.000	$36.000

As for property 2, appreciation will be $20.000 (10 years * 2% * 100.000 initial worth) and the net rental income will be $36.000 ($300 * 12 months * 10 years), which means a combined total of $56.000. If the investor is able to get a very high return on the $100 monthly difference, then property 2 can be a better investment.

However, note that getting a return equal to the difference between the appreciation rates (4% - 2% = 2%) is not enough. Getting this 2% rate on the difference in net rental income ($100 in this case) would only result in a total of $240, after the 10 year period! Do the math yourself: $100 * 12 months * 2% * 10 years = $240. This is because while the 2% appreciation difference is based on the initial property worth ($100.000 in this case), we are talking about a small difference of $100 between the rental income of the properties. Therefore, for this model to work, the investor should either need the money (if the money is needed for other purposes this is even not up to discussion) or be able to get a much higher return on the extra cash every month.

The most practical way of doing that is to invest the extra cash in assets that appreciate a lot. For instance, if the investor applies the $1.200 yearly difference in net rental income towards other properties, which also appreciate 2% every year, then the situation changes tremendously; at the end of the first year, in the case the investor went with property 2, he can now use the "extra" $1.200 as a down payment to buy another property, property 3. These will be invested towards taxes and fees, and the investor is 100% financed on the property itself, so let's just assume the $1.200 are "lost". However, if we are talking about a property that is worth the same $100.000 and appreciates 2% every year, then the investor will profit $18.000 (9 years * $100.000 * 2%) in appreciation alone. That is still a good scenario (from a financial standpoint) even if the rental income only covers taxes, maintenance and the mortgage payments.

In this example, the investor would have profited $20.000 in appreciation on property 2 (10 years * 2% * $100.000 initial worth), a total of $36.000 ($300 * 12 months * 10 years) in gross rental income. From these, $1.200 would be used for the down payment of property 3, and $18.000 ($100.000 * 2% * 9 years) of appreciation on property 3, thus summing up to a final total of $74.000 ($20.000 + $36.000 + $18.000).

Please note that in these calculations I have put things in very simple terms, since it would be complicated to elaborate on the financials behind these operations. For instance, I haven't considered compound appreciation, equity and debt, inflation or even capital gains for appreciation, which would change the scenario. However, the goal of this section is to show the differences – simply from a financial standpoint, i.e. not considering risk – between the models. Later on, I will give examples where other variables are also factored in, so we can study them as well.

Risk and advantages of having more capital early on

There are many advantages to this method, which I do not have the space in this book to fully go through. However, having capital sooner and diluting risk is an advantage way too important not to talk about it.

Unlike the appreciation-based model, which I will cover next, this model allows the investor to buy real estate properties sooner, because the return of capital is faster and it can be used as a down payment for more properties. This allows the investor to dilute the risk of the investments.

At the same time, the fact that capital is gotten back faster has two other clear advantages: 1) first, it brings the investor emotional comfort, 2) second, it increases liquidity, something very important in any investment, including real estate. Liquidity is essential to take up any good opportunity that pops up in the market. If you allocate all of your capital, you will miss any good opportunity that may arise.

Appreciation-based model

This model is pretty much the opposite to the cash flow maximization model. In this model, investors focus on acquiring properties that are expected to appreciate considerably over time, instead of having high yields. These properties are usually in fast-growing markets, markets that can benefit from growing neighborhoods or considerable investments in the area, or markets that are temporarily down and are predicted to recover.

In this model, there is no concern with high yields, in the short term. This is a more passive model, in the sense that investors who follow this model tend to focus on investing in the right market and not the right property, and do not really worry if rents are moderate; time will do more than anything else for investors, in this model.

Your own model

In the previous sections, I have introduced both ends of the spectrum of real estate investing models. They are just that – ends of a spectrum. Between these two models, there are many different combinations you can follow. The most important thing is to be aware of the advantages and disadvantages of each model, thus knowing which one fits your investment profile, strategy and vision the best.

I have personally always followed a pure cash flow maximization model, ever since I started my own physical portfolio. This is because I'd rather have cash today than appreciation tomorrow. However, I have always been able to get a decent return on capital, that surpassed the gains of generic real estate appreciation (in the markets I buy real estate). Additionally, this model suits my strategy and vision better. In your own case, you should give this a deep thought and assess what model suits you the best.

The importance of goals

"Your goal must be big. Shoot for the moon. Even if you miss, you'll land among the stars.". One of my favorite quotes. The first thing that any investor who wants to invest in the long term (versus making a quick buck) should have is a vision – so big that it should reach the stars.

Setting goals is of prime importance for every decent sized vision, in order to maximize the chances of success. I set goals for myself and my company every quarter, and then I split them into monthly goals. Usually I do not set goals for more than 90 days because it is proven that those become unrealistic pretty quickly. The only thing that goes after the 90 days is your vision.

As for the personal goals – which have to do with money, health, social and personal aspects – those were the essence of my success until today. I recommend every one of my friends to have them, because they are essential in the personal development and reaching success, in my opinion. I would practice them at the personal level and then at the business and investment level, that is my most generic advice. It has worked for me until today, I hope it works for you too.

Dividir para conquistar - divide and conquer

Divide and conquer – break goals down into stages. This is probably the most efficient way of maximizing the chances of executing your strategy successfully, and reach your vision. Have you ever thought that, in order to become a millionaire in 20 years, you need to make $50.000 per year, which is about $4.000 per month or $1.000 per week? Making $1.000 per week may be difficult for a lot of people, but it certainly looks easier than becoming a millionaire. Divide goals – to conquer – is a proven process in our lives.

For instance, when I co-founded ArrowPlus, my company, I had the vision that I would help all investors in my country that wanted to invest in real estate. I said we would help them in a very pragmatic, easy, accessible and efficient way. For instance, we do market surveys, which usually cost dozens of thousands of bucks, for less than a thousand bucks. And a lot of other goals were set, so that we could reach the final vision we have for the company.

All in all, what I am telling you is that you should have a vision. Invest some time into it, realize what it represents to you and why you want to reach it. Then, choose a strategy and a model that suit your investment profile. And lastly, set goals and help you to execute the chosen model with success.

4

Financing

Leveraging (i.e. financing operations) is one of the biggest advantages of real estate investing, in my opinion. Real Estate offers the possibility of financing investments as no other type of investment, as I said in the first chapter. This is one of the most important factors in real estate investing, because it allows virtually everyone to invest.

This chapter goes over the various angles of financing, in the context of real estate investing.

Banks

Banks offer the most traditional financing methods there are, since a long time. In some countries, such as the US, there are specialize lenders, such as mortgage brokers. Both provide almost universal access and the process is standardized and simple. Additionally, today we can obtain multiple mortgage simulations online and most real estate companies work with directly with mortgage brokers, which increases the speed and chances of getting an answer to a possible loan, at the same time the process becomes easier and more convenient.

Banks and mortgage brokers offer different loans (including different rates, such as fixed, adjustable, mixed, fixed installments, etc). The reality in your country may vary a lot from other countries; while in my country, Portugal, Adjustable Rate Mortgages (ARMs) are the vast majority of mortgages settled, in the US fixed-rate mortgages tend to be more popular and ARMs are no more than 10% of all mortgages. ARMs can be cheaper in the short-term but way more expensive in the long run. Therefore, they may not be the most intelligent option, depending on the circumstances, as I will show you in the next section. This section shows the types of loans investors can get from banks and mortgage brokers to invest in real estate.

Mortgage loans

Mortgage loans are the most conventional method of getting a loan to invest in real estate.

As I said before, banks in general look at two indicators when assessing a loan: a guarantee that covers the amount of the loan, for a given LTV (which is why the property is given as a collateral in the security interest) and a good indicator of financial capability. The latter is a financial plan that is solid enough so that the mortgage installments do not represent a large effort to the debtor, as a function of his income.

If an individual asks for a loan as an individual (and not as a company) his salary is typically the most important thing in the assessment of the creditworthiness of the individual. Plus, lenders will assess not only how large the income is, but also its "quality", i.e. how predictable and "safe" that income is over time.

Investors can also ask for loans as a company (typically an LLC), something I talk about in the next chapter.

A very important subject in the context of mortgage loans is the type of rate and amount of time the loan spans over. As for the time, it has primarily to do with your age, strategy and rental income on that property. However, the most important subject is the type of rate, which I discuss next.

Interest rates: adjustable vs fixed

As I just told you, there are a few things to decide when going with a mortgage loan, such us its length (which is not fully up to you, the lender will certainly provide a maximum period). However, the most important decision you will have to make, in my opinion, is choosing the type of interest rate of the loan: adjustable or fixed.

Depending on where you live, one of these may be way more popular than the other. For instance, in Portugal – where I come from, adjustable rates are far more popular than fixed rates. In the US, adjustable rates currently represent under 10% of all mortgages in the country.

Adjustable interest rates (also called floating rates) are usually composed of two different components in Europe: the "spread" and the "Euribor". Euribor is, put simply, a reference rate for loans between some European banks. Therefore, you cannot negotiate the Euribor rate with the bank, only the spread. Banks may use 3/6/12-month Euribor, which may change every 3, 6 or 12 months. The spread rate is defined by the bank and you can therefore negotiate it (see Chapter 6 – Negotiate with banks). Note than the spread rate the bank will propose you stems from the risk of lending you money (including guarantees and financial capability), based on the property to be bought, the amount of the loan, your income (and type of income), etc. When the Euribor rate increases a lot, it has been a common practice for the banks to negotiate the spread rate - otherwise there are many people who may default on their mortgages – but banks do not have to do it.

In the US, the system works pretty differently. Euribor is not used in the US, where mortgages are either fixed-rate or adjustable-rate (ARMs). ARMs come in different forms: 3/1 ARMs, 7/1 ARMs and 10/1 ARMs, which have fixed rates for 3, 7 and 10 years respectively. If you wonder why the /"1", that means the rate can change every year. Now, ARMs in the US also have two components: the index (interest rate), which ARMs move up and down with, and the margin. The index is an interest rate set by the market, and is the analog of the Euribor rate in Europe. However, there are indexes, and each ARM may follow a different one. The margin is added by the bank, and it is the equivalent to the spread in Europe.

The fixed interest rate is different from the adjustable one because it does not change during the entire period of the loan. ARMs may have a period where the rate is fixed as I said, but fixed rate mortgages have the same rate throughout the entire period. Thus, this rate is not affected by indexes, such as Euribor and others. You may think that fixed rates may always be more advantageous than adjustable rates, but fixed-rates pay a premium, and therefore they are usually a higher than the adjustable rates, when the loan starts. In fact, the lender is assuming a risk, because although the bank lends you money at a given rate, the bank has no guarantee it will be financed itself at a lower or even the same rate (yes, banks also borrow money).

Now that I have explained the difference between both rates, we should discuss which one is best. Naturally, the answer depends upon many factors, and I believe that it will never be an universal answer, as it is tightly connected to the context in which you are in. That is, there are so many factors involved (such as your investing profile, type of investment, market, type of property, expected appreciation, etc), that it is impossible to say what is the best type of rate for each investor, or even each deal.

Personally, in general, I prefer fixed-rate mortgages to invest in real estate. However, that does not mean that is the best decision for your own investments. The reasons why I personally prefer fixed rates are:

1. **Passiveness of my portfolio**. This may sound odd at first, but let me explain. If you get ARMs, be prepared to make adjustments to your portfolio, in the long term (this is especially true for large portfolios – small

portfolios will in general have little exposure so this makes a big difference). This is because as the rates rise, your liquidity decreases, which will force you to make adjustments as the Euribor/index rates raise. As I planned my portfolio to be as passive as possible, I believe that I will not need to make big adjustments in a 30-, 40- or even 50-year horizon. Of course that this is a very long time span, and a lot of things may change, thus changing my perspective of my portfolio as well. However, I make decisions based on the variables I know when I make them, and they assume a given projection (as realistic as possible) to the future. The same logic is actually often employed by successful investors, to other investments. For the stock market, for instance, many successful investors invest as if the market was to be closed for the 10 following years.

2. **It makes it easy to assess other deals**. I go with fixed rates (let us suppose 4% - a realistic rate as of today - for the sake of discussion) because it makes it easy for me to assess subsequent deals, including to determine whether they are good or not. For example, a 3% yield deal only makes sense if I can finance it at less than 3%, or I have been financing other deals at less than 3%. However, with adjustable rates that is simply too hard to predict: today, e.g. Euribor is close to 0% but in the future it is expected to raise – I personally predict a final adjustable rate of 5% in the next years. I make many deals that I need to close fast, and I need to determine whether they make sense to my portfolio (based on the rates I finance my deals and the yields that I have). Thus, knowing exactly at what rate I am financing a deal throughout the entire period of that investment is absolutely crucial for me.

3. **Safety/solid financial planning.** Later on in this book, I will talk about "bullet proof models", because I believe that real estate portfolios have to be planned in such a way that they are profitable but also sold in the long run. This is why I prefer to finance deals with a fixed rate. Essentially, liquidly

and installments to pay off that both vary way too much with adjustable rate mortgages. Most likely, for a small portfolio composed of one or two properties that will not change the grand scheme of things. However, in a decent sized portfolio, this may mean dozens or hundreds of thousands of bucks of additional debt, for a given year. I will talk about risk mitigation in this regard, later on, however this is a risk investors will never be able to completely eliminate; even if you could have your rental income vary with the index of your mortgages (imagine telling that to a tenant…), the interest to pay would – most likely – much higher than the increase in the rental income.

In Chapter 6, I present several tips and methods that you can use when negotiating with banks.

Prepayments (also called prepays)

There is another very important subject within the realm of mortgages: prepayments. First, most mortgages include prepayment penalties (some borrowers are so eager to close on their mortgages, they gloss over this subject, only to have a negative surprise a few years later, when they consider a prepayment). Prepayments vary a lot. In Europe, ARMs usually have a 0.5% (half percent) prepayment penalty on the current debt, and fixed-rate mortgages usually have a 2% prepayment penalty, but this varies among countries and even banks and types of mortgages. In the US, lenders usually consider two types of prepayment penalties, soft and hard. Soft prepayment penalties usually allow borrowers to walk away with no penalty should they sell their home (and pay off the entire loan) and do not refinance (if they refinance, they usually incur a prepayment penalty). Hard prepayment penalties include a penalty either if borrowers sell their house or refinance. The good thing about the system in the US, is that prepays only last for a few years after the loan started, while in Europe they are applied until the end of the loan. Also, in the US, they are usually 80% of six months interest (and interest only). In both systems, prepays are proportionally more expensive in the beginning of the loan. That makes sense because prepays exist to protect the lenders, which are usually not interested in prepays as they will make less profit on the loan.

The most important question when it comes to prepays, in the context of real estate investing, is whether an investor should prepay a mortgage. As time went by and I got more and more experienced in real estate investing and I contacted with more and more clients, I needed to come up with a generic thumb rule to answer to this question pragmatically. I will provide you with this simple rule I devised for myself and I will explain why I believe it is effective. Let us assume the scenario where an investor has all the capital needed to make a certain investment. Most people would pay the property all cash, since they have the money anyway. However, there are two scenarios where I personally see merit in financing a deal, even when an investor has the capital for it:

1. The investor can get **a return on his cash at a higher rate** than what he interest rate he will pay on the debt (e.g., the interest rate of mortgage). For example, if the investor has a 10% yield (on another property or an investment outside of real estate) and he/she "only" pays 3% interest on his/her debt, then it is generally profitable to finance the deal and invest his/her own capital, because there is a positive difference of 7%.

2. The property that is being acquired will have an **expected yield rate that is higher** than the interest rate to be paid on the debt. For example, if a given property yields 8% of the total investment, and the investor "only" pays 4% interest on his/her debt, then – based on considering this alone – it makes sense to finance the deal. The logic is thus very simple: when the investor's own capital yields a higher rate than the debt's rate, then it is generally better to finance new deals.

Note that this – very simplified – model does not factor in non-financial aspects, such as liquidity, portfolio changes, prepays, etc.

At the same time, there is a very simple model to determine when it is better for the investor to prepay his/her debt:

1. If the investor is not able to get a return rate on his/her own money that is higher than the interest rate on his/her debt (consider the net margins).
2. If the property net yield becomes higher than the net interest rate on the debt (again, always consider net margins).

Note that this model does not factor in the costs that decrease when prepaying a mortgage (for instance, life insurance costs associated with the mortgage) and another very important – yet not financial aspect – subject: the total amount of debt. The total amount of debt is particularly important because it may allow the investor to finance other/more deals. Sometimes, it may make sense to prepay a given mortgage just so that lenders become willing to lend more money. This may sound odd, but I have seen several examples where investors increased their creditworthiness by $100.000 if they were to prepay $20.000 on an existing mortgage. This is because sometimes the creditworthiness assessment is done by brackets, such as number of mortgages or total amount of debt, and therefore it is sometimes possible that a small reduction in a given mortgage allows the investor to qualify for another loan.

Lines of credit

Experienced real estate investors require other financing tools, as mortgage loans become quite limited. Investors can, for instance, resort to lines of credit. Lines of credit may have a myriad of names and forms, depending on the country, bank, lender and purpose. For instance, in the US they can be dubbed Investment Property Line of Credit (LOC), Home Equity Line of Credit (HELOC), among others. Note that each type of line of credit may have different terms, and even the same type of line of credit may have different terms among different banks. In Europe, they run under the names of Line of Credit (LOC), Generic Mortgage (GM), among others.

They are all different and take different forms and terms, but their generic process is the same (or similar, at least). In the context of real estate, a line of credit allows access to a specific amount of financing, within a certain period (referred to as term) and it is secured by property equity (and/or other assets, provided as collateral).

It is important to say that lines of credit work very differently among countries and therefore you should always consult your bank account manager about this issue. I will provide a general description of lines of credit based on what my experience is, having lived in different countries and having read about lines of credit from different sources. Take this section as a general description of lines of credit and check with your local lenders whether they have a similar model.

There are different lines of credit, but we can look at them as an agreement with a lender, made ahead of time, that almost forces the lender to lend you money, according to the agreed terms. There are secured and unsecured lines of credit, but I would like to cover secured lines of credit, as they are the most relevant in this context. Most lines of credit in the context of real estate investing (such as HELOCs) are secured by the property the debtor has. The property is then the collateral the lender can seize if the debtor defaults on the line of credit. The maximum amount of credit is set based on the property's worth (usually, with considering a given LTV).

HELOCs work pretty similarly to this generic model: you just had your house appraised and its work came out at $135.000. Let us assume you have a balance due on the mortgage of to $50.000. This results in a home equity of $85.000, which you can borrow against – this would be a home equity loan, i.e. a lump sum, not a line of credit. A line of credit would, in general, be calculated as follows: assuming a 70% LTV (this varies a lot from lender to lender), the lender would be willing to lend you 70% * $135.000 = $94.500, but since you have a balance due of $50.000, then you could only tap into $44.500. In fact, you could borrow up to $44.500 and tap into it as you would need it.

Lines of credit – in any form – are a very important tool in the context of real estate investing, especially for large transactions. Here are the most important reasons why I think this is the case:

1. ***Lines of credit allow for quick access to capital.*** They allow the investor to tap into capital easier than asking for a mortgage loan at each property that is bought. There are two reasons for this: first, you already have the asset/home to borrow against, and you may already know or have a very good idea of how much it is worth; second, after the line of credit is settled, money is quickly deposited in your account once you request it.

2. ***They allow investors to look for deals knowing they will be financed.*** If you go out there shopping for properties, you are not sure the bank will lend you the money you need to finance the deal. Yes, you may get a pre-approval from a lender, but a pre-approval is not an approval (meaning the lender may actually end up not lend you the money based on the property you require the loan for) and offers on properties will be conditioned (while offers based on lines of credit are usually taken more seriously, because you can in fact tap into the credit). Later on I will show you ways to mitigate the uncertainty of having a loan when needed.

As for companies (in the next chapter, I will present you the advantages and disadvantages of creating a company to invest in real estate, in detail), these operations are actually easier, because the company's revenue is usually more consistent and lenders have various different programs to fund companies. Again, this is highly dependent on the country you are in and I advise you to talk to your account manager and ask him more on this (see more on Chapter 6).

Business partners

Financing with banks and lenders is the most standard way to finance a deal, but it is not necessarily the best one. Buying real estate with business partners is an alternative to that, and offers several advantages, such as:

3. ***It is way easier...*** after you find a business partner. Although finding a business partner may be tough, especially for investors who are taking the first steps in real estate investing, the process of financing is very simple, once the business partnership is established. The process is simple because the terms and the relationship are already settled, and the variables are known upfront.

4. ***It is more flexible.*** Do you only have 30% of the capital to close the next awesome deal? All you need to do is to find a partner who puts up the other 70%. And this is way more appealing than it may actually sound. Imagine you are to start investing, and you only have 15% of the capital required to close a new deal. Finding a business partner will allow you to start investing sooner than later. But this is a two sided equation, so you may also raise the legitimate question of whether you can benefit from having a business partner if you have the capital, but not the time to find good investments and manage the properties. If that is the case, you can try to find a partner who has the time and the skills, and lacks the capital.

5. ***There are no commissions.*** In contrast to lenders, which have to appraise the properties and charge you for that, together with other commissions (altogether this is known as "closing costs"), this does not happen when you have a business partner. Of course you can also borrow money, together with a business partner, and in that case you will have closing costs to pay, but you may still benefit from that because the lenders will consider both yours and your business partner's income. Finally, please consider that when you have a loan, there are

taxes on the loan as well, which can be avoided if you find a partner who finances the deals.

However, finding business partners is not all roses. If you do not know the person who you will have a business partnership, this may become a problem, for obvious reasons. Plus, if you finance a deal together with a business partner, please be aware that in many countries the total debt will be both partner's responsibility. This means that if you buy a $100.000 property with a business partner and you finance the operation, each partner will owe $50.000 but both will be the guarantors of the other $50.000.

In some countries, opening up a company to hold real estate is very expensive and usually does not pay off unless there is a number of properties to hold in the company. Depending on your country's legislation, you may not have to open a company to invest with a business partner. Some countries allow multiple individuals to own real estate together, without the need to create a company to hold the real estate (and then assign the company's shares to the partners). The countries that allow this typically assign different parts of the property to different people. This is something that you need to check depending on where you live.

Finding business partners

Although there are several advantages to this, finding partners is generally a tough nut to crack. I myself have tried to find business partners back in the day, so I know how tough this can be. It was easy for me to find people willing to invest, but they had no capital for access to credit. It was also especially tough to find partners that were physically close to me (so it would be easier to create a relationship and get to know people).

Crowdfunding platforms democratized the access to business partners. Have you ever heard of Kickstarter? It is a platform to find people willing to finance your company (usually by purchasing a given product at an attractive price). There are similar platforms for real estate investing; it is possible to create a campaign for a particular deal, and wait for partners to join you on that venture. If you find good fix and flip deals, these platforms may be just what you are looking for.

There are also companies that specialize in connecting business partners. Although my company does not offer that as a service, it has happened, by accident, that two different clients invested together and became partners.

If you start investing in real estate, it will be easier to find business opportunities and business partners; in fact, since I am in business (as an individual, not through ArrowPlus) and I have proven to be trustworthy, I have been approached by many people with all kinds of proposals. I believe the same will happen to you, should you be open to that.

Other financing methods

If the two last types of financing does not please you or are not accessible to you, do not become disapointed, because there are more options available.

The first is raising money through family and friends. Personally, I have never done this, but I have several friend who have (I have actually financed some of their projects myself). This loan model can actually be extended to more people, including the property seller himself (this type of deal is called seller-financed). Other loans (which are often more accessible, but come with higher interest rates) include personal credits or getting loans from individual lenders.

The second way to finance a real estate deal is through venture capital or angle investors. This is usually not the first type of investment angles and venture capital investors look for, but I have seen deals like this going through. Usually, these type of investors look for very high returns on their money (most of the time, at the cost of high risk). Therefore, to be financed this way, you will need a long-term plan that convinces the angle investor of a very large return on his money. In the context of real estate deals, this is easier (should I call it not as hard?) to achieve with fix and flips deals.

The third option is to resort to crowdfunding platforms, as I said before. Usually, these platforms are also more geared towards fix and flip, since investors look for short term returns. Other platforms allow investors to finance themselves with Peer to Peer (P2P) loans – i.e. loans provided directly by other individuals or lending companies. In these platforms, the interest rate is usually higher than through other channels.

5

Other financial aspects

In order to optimize real estate investing, there are several financial aspects that must be taken into account. Beyond what I explained in the previous chapter, which pertain mostly to property financing, it is necessary to structure investments in a certain way, if the goal is to optimize the investment for taxes, logistics and safety. Taxes are almost always unavoidable, but the tax code often provides different taxation ways, with very different ending results, so you should choose what works best for you, within the realm of legality. Logistics are a big topic in real estate and may be one of the most optimizable parts of real estate investing. As for the safety of your investment, please note first and foremost that all investments have risk involved; however, there are things we can do to make our investments safer.

In this chapter I will talk about these 3 vectors, from a financial standpoint.

Invest through a company vs as an individual

One of the major questions that those who are taking the first steps in real estate investing, is whether they should invest through a company/holding or as an individual (also referred to as a sole-trader). This is a very complex question that must be raised for each specific case. I recommend you always assess this question together with a licensed accountant and a lawyer. In fact, their advice is one of the most important parts of building a real estate portfolio – big or small –, in my opinion. However, even if I recommend always assessing this question with an accountant and a lawyer. this is a question I could simply leave unaddressed in this book.

There are several advantages to setting up a company to invest in real estate, as I have done myself. However, the actual advantages depend on what country you are in. For instance, in my country, the biggest advantage of a real estate holding pertains to tax optimization. In other countries, the legal part is considerably more relevant than in Portugal, because it is more common that landlords are sued by tenants. Having all this in mind, take the following generic comparison with a pinch of salt. As this book was adapted so that is was not bounded to the reality of a specific country, always consider the context in your own country.

The tax angle has different nuances, and that is another reason to discuss this with your licensed accountant. However, I always point out generic advantages of setting up a company to invest in real estate. Also, make sure that there are several different types of companies to do this, including Limited Liability Companies (LLC), Limited Liability Partnerships (LLP) – which usually fall under the same rules of sole sole-traders, investment companies, trading companies and we could even consider pension schemes. Again, in your country, there may exist different company structures available;

This being said, setting up companies to invest in real estate usually have two main advantages:

1. ***For companies, taxes are usually either lower or offer more room for optimization.*** This is in fact so relevant that I have seen many investors framing their real estate investment structures as companies solely on tax benefits. In many countries, it is not allowed to write off mortgage interest against rental income if the rentals are owned individually (versus through a company). Also, the tax code for individuals in some countries does not allow to write off expenses that are not directly related to obtaining rental income, such as travels (even if business travels), however this is allowed if the company holds the real estate itself. There are also countries where companies have taxation brackets of their own, and countries where the revenue (and losses) of the companies pass through its members. In many countries, including the US, there are differences in taxation depending on whether the LLC has one or more members, so you must check that carefully.

2. ***Companies offer limited personal vulnerability.*** LLCs and LLC-alike structures usually limit personal vulnerability to potential lawsuits that may exist in the context of the rental properties. In most countries, if real estate is held by the company, then the company is responsible for the lawsuit, and not the individual(s) who own(s) the company. This means that, in case of a lawsuit, the investor's own assets could not be touched or seized. However, note that all the assets of the company could be seized in the context of that lawsuit, which is often why we see professional investors creating one LLC per real estate deal.

This brings me to the next point. Although there are several and clear advantages in creating a company to invest in real estate, that does not mean companies are the right choice for every investor, and some investors may actually prefer to invest as individuals. Also, if you live in a country where the law is much more in favor of landlords than tenants, the legal aspect of setting up a company to invest in real estate is not as important. Or say you live in a country where taxation is pretty similar for both companies and individuals, in the context of real estate. And there are more variables. Maybe you live in a place where liability insurance is very affordable and you believe it is better to take well-covering insurance rather than setting an LLC.

However, the main reason why an LLC (or any other company structure, for that matter) is usually not a first option for many real estate investors is because their logistic costs are too high if the real estate portfolio is small. Although the costs incurred with the creation and maintenance of a company depend on how the company is run, there are costs that seem to exist in most countries:

1. *There are filling rates*. Setting up a company costs money in most countries in the world, and it seems be vary from as little as $50 to as much as $5000. Depending on the size of the portfolio, this may or may not be significant. In the US, this costs varies considerably among different states.

2. *You need to pay for an accountant/bookkeeper, and yearly fees*. Again, the reality is different in many countries but for some of them, you will need to hire an accountant/bookkeeper. In Portugal, many accountants charge a minimum regardless of the work involved in the company, while in many countries like the US, bookkeepers tend to charge solely based on the amount of work there is. This is relevant because if you only buy one or two properties, it may pay off to set an LLC in the US but not e.g. in Portugal. Some bookkeepers will factor in the tax return, others do not. As for yearly fees, they may or may not be a reality in your own country. In 2017, some sources report that the average LLC yearly fee among the various states in the US was $101 (some actually have no yearly fees).

3. *Insurance, licenses and other fees*. The universal advice is to take insurance for your company, but this topic is so broad and different

from country to country that is may make sense to go without insurance if you are only using the company to invest in real estate. However, in some countries, there are mandatory insurances. Also, if you intend to do business other than holding and renting out real estate (if you open the company to set up a buy-and-hold portfolio), then you will not need any licenses. However, please factor in fees that you will have to pay, including bank fees.

4. *Annual taxes*. In some countries, single-owned LLCs are viewed by the IRS as sole proprietorships for tax purposes. If this is the case, then the profits or gains on the company pass through the owner, who then reposts them on his tax return, therefore paying taxes there. For multiple-owned LLCs, some countries may pass through the different owners, while other countries have specific income tax brackets for companies. Always discuss this matter with a licensed accountant.

5. *Salaries*. Typically around the world you have two ways of getting money from your own company: through a salary or dividends. If you pay yourself a salary you may need to factor in social security, 401k, and retirement pension contributions, and you may have to take health insurance, all of which are costs to the company.

Although these costs are pretty much mandatory and can sum up to hundreds of bucks a month, there are other optional costs that may make sense incurring. These include, among others:

1. *Legal advice/counseling*. If you are making a direct comparison between holding real estate as an individual versus a company, then I do not see why it would be more expensive to have legal advice through a company, but note that you may need to hire a lawyer to answer on legal issues of the company itself. For instance, many people hire a

lawyer to set up a company. Of course you would not incur this cost if you were to invest in real estate as an individual.

2. ***Facilities or locations***. Again, if you are using a company solely to invest in real estate, in theory you have no reason to have a location to serve clients. However, this may be a possibility in order to attract more tenants, or at least quicker. Check whether you need any license to do this in your area (in most countries, you will need no license if you only look out for tenants for your own properties).

3. ***Insurance***. I have covered this above, but I want to emphasize that, in some countries, there may be mandatory insurance just because you set up a company.

Then there is typically a bunch of optional costs, which you should also consider when setting up a company:

1. ***Vehicles.*** You may need to buy a car. It is not because you set up a company that you will need a car, but know that in some countries you may actually write off (a percentage of) the car cost or lease .

2. ***Advertisement***. You may want to advertise your real estate (e.g. running ads on digital platforms). However, this should not be more expensive because you set up a company (versus individuals).

3. ***Employees***. Same thing, investing through a company will not increase your needs at this level. But, if you do hire employees, you need to factor in contributions of social security, health insurance, etc, depending on what your local legislation determines. I have had contact with clients of my company who set up a company to invest in real estate. Although they hired property management companies in the beginning, as their portfolio grew, they ended up hiring employees to manage their own properties.

REITs versus a physical portfolio

As I showed you in the previous section, actively invest in real estate can have some costs. More than the costs incurred, the investor has quite some responsibility and, as any active investment, managing an investment requires time. In fact, I believe that managing a real estate portfolio takes more time than most other investments. We must keep in mind that, among other things, it is necessary to be in regular synchrony with tenants, who may complain often, ensure that maintenance is done (which also involves getting quotes for all kinds of problems), finding new tenants, check the payment of rents (and notify tenants when necessary), etc...

Investing in real estate can quickly become a time-consuming activity. One or two properties are easy to manage, especially if you are physically close to them. However, as you grow your portfolio, the time necessary to manage it increases (in my experience more than linearly). Active management is actually one of the main reasons why investors do not succeed in real estate – they underestimate the time necessary to control a portfolio. It is also the main reason why many investors across other types of investments do not like real estate.

This is why many investors who find real estate a good investment end up investing through REITs. REITs are a very interesting way to invest in real estate because:

1. ***They are very liquid***. REITs allow investors to buy and sell stake in real estate in a very easy and quick way, while remaining liquid. It is considerably easier to sell REIT stake than selling real estate directly – at least the second it will take way longer (on average).

2. ***They are diversified***. When an investor buys shares of a given REIT, he is buying the equivalent to a set of real estate properties. In practice, this means that the investor is actually investing in many different markets (possibly different countries) as well as different types of real estate properties and with different allocations (commercial, residential, etc).

This being said, REITs have some cons as well, which include:

1. ***Lack of control – the investor cannot decide what to do with the properties***. Let us say you believe the market is at a top and is going to correct. You would like to sell, because this would generate a nice profit. This will not happen with a REIT because investors do not determine the course of the REIT, plus REITs are usually run with a long-term perspective.

2. ***Margins are typically lower***. As with every investments, there is a trade-off between how active/time consuming the investment is and its potential. For instance, you can simply pour money into a REIT, sit back and enjoy your profits, while that will not happen with physical real estate (if you simply buy the properties you will probably lose money).

Each investor must determine what makes sense for his/her own case. If you bought this book and you want to invest, you are probably looking to get the larger margins possible, by actively investing in real estate. In fact, this book was written having that type of investors in mind – as you can easily observe through the next chapters – although I wrote it so that everyone could benefit from it. However, active management of real estate is not necessarily the best alternative for all investors, as some investors simply want to allocate some capital and are willing to have lower returns if they come with no headaches.

Emergency fund

Growing a portfolio or simply investing in real estate increases your responsibility. I have personally been confronted with the urgent need to replace a roof, and the day before that the roof was perfect.

This setback is an example among many. Real estate investing can be a safe, profitable and interesting method to accumulate wealth. Do not take it from me, take it from history and well known real estate investors. However, unlike stocks or bonds, you may have to pour money into your properties when you are not expecting it.

I always recommend my clients to set up an emergency fund, and I recommend that to you as well. Usually, as an analyst, I typically recommended to set up a liquid (either cash or cash-equivalent) emergency fund of 1%-2% of the total portfolio's worth. That means, for a $500.000 portfolio, I would recommend to have an emergency fund of $5.000 to $10.000, but you will have to determine what makes sense in your own case. To set up this fund in the beginning, when cash flow is more limited, I personally allocated 10% of the monthly collected rents to this fund, at this has worked for me. But remember, your expenses may go well beyond what your emergency fund is capable of covering. I personally look to is as a buffer that will help me if a setback arises – not as an instrument to solve all my problems.

6

Negotiating with lenders

Before you actually go shopping for real estate and start negotiating properties, unless you have got all the capital you need, you should first negotiate with lenders, such as banks. The majority of people think that banks are standardized machines where we can only get what is provided. But tell me tell you a very important secret: everything is negotiable, even at banks and lenders. And when I say "everything", I mean "everything". Banks are financial institutions, which, from a business standpoint, are not that different from the other businesses (the biggest expectation being that they are highly regulated).

Banks sell products and services and what to make a profit, simple. As such, they want to get new clients all the time (just like any other business), and bank and branch managers actually get bonuses based sometimes on the number of new clients their location has gotten in a given month.

In fact, the goals that banks and lenders set are of prime importance to any investor. This may in fact be a window of opportunity to many investors. Have you heard the saying "when you owe the bank 1 million, you have got a problem, when you owe the bank 100 million the bank has a problem?". But that is the bank's problem. Investors should try to explore – as much as legally and ethically as possible – any bank's policies to his/her own favor. I always negotiate with banks based on their policies. If I know they have some goals (say lend a specific amount of get X new clients) that quarter, and I use that to my favor, I do not see why I should not. Plus, banks have specific product campaigns every now and then. For instance, on a specific month they want to increase their loans, to meet some target, and they lower their rates/margins.

As I said before, I like fixed-rates, and I have shown you some reasons why. Usually banks (especially in Portugal) charge way more in fixed-rate loans than they do in adjustable. I am not talking about the premium that fixed-rates have. I am saying that banks price that premium way too high, especially when compared to other countries like the US. But this can also be used to my advantage: if they have better margins, they have more room for negotiation, right? This is what I do across the board: I choose my favorite products the banks have, I estimate their margins, and I negotiate based on that. However, what I will teach you in this chapter can be used for any kind of negotiation.

Rates and terms of mortgage loans

For any investor, mortgage loans are really the most important product the bank has to offer. This is typically how any investor starts leveraging. Many lenders are specialized in mortgage loans. That is what they do best and the type of business they want to do, because of their margins, process, etc.

To start the process, the investor should select a set of banks and lenders he/she wants to work with. You should be open to work with any bank, given that any bank may have the best rates and terms, but you should start off with a set of them, based on things like how close you are to their locations/branches, the type of history that you have with a bank, whether the bank has an ongoing campaign (which means better terms) on a specific loan you want, etc.

I would like to emphasize the history that you have with the bank, before moving further. In the US, there is the credit score, which essentially measures one's creditworthiness. In most European countries, there is no similar system; banks determine clients' creditworthiness by assessing their income and their current debt. Whenever debtors default on credit, there is no such thing as a credit score that decreases, instead the default is marked in a centralized (usually run by each country's national bank) as that. Banks can know what is the current debt of a given debtor and whether the debtor ever defaulted on any credit.

Your history before a bank is so important that it is actually common for some investors to create credit history on purpose, before asking for a loan. In the US, this is actually done with "secure loans", i.e. loans that are secured by some collateral – most often money. In Europe, it is more common to max out credit cards and make sure that the credit card bill is paid on time. Prepays can be taken as something positive (as the client proves to be capable of generating liquidity) or negative (because banks typically "lose" money when clients prepay), but such assessment is done individually by each bank. In fact, one may look very creditworthiness before a given bank and not creditworthy at all before another.

Today, most creditworthiness assessment is done with computers, which run algorithms that determine such a thing. People (bankers) only jump in at the end of the process. Think about it. Have you ever simulated a mortgage loan with a banker? He may have told you that "the system (computer) only provides such a margin...". That is because the algorithms that run your data will determine the risk of you defaulting and based on that they provide the best terms of a loan. My advice is – if you are serious about leveraging, make sure you have some history (or work on your credit, if you are in the US) before asking for it, as this step can improve your odds of qualify for a loan and the rates of a possible loan altogether.

OK, now that you have selected a set of banks/lenders and you have worked on your credit – possibly through credit cards or secured loans (look at this step as you showing the bank you can take on some debt), the next step is to determine which of those banks will offer you – without any negotiation – the best terms and rates...

Get multiple offers

The first thing I recommend, if you are thinking about financing a real estate deal, is to get multiple offers for a mortgage loan (or any loan for that matter). Today, you can actually get quotes and simulations online, at no cost, and from my experience they are in line with the offers you will end up getting from a bank if you ask for a formal offer at a physical location/branch. Thus, you can start this process at home: select a few banks you want to work with and ask for a few simulations/quotes.

This is a very important part of my strategy, because there are two points that have been particularly fruitful when negotiating with banks: 1) the possibility of becoming a client of that bank/lender and 2) have a better offer from another bank, which I can use to my own favor.

Now, the second step of my negotiation strategy is to select the second best offer/quote and negotiate that one in person, at the bank. You may be wondering why I said "the second best" and not the best. But what I do is to show that bank that there are better offers in the market. Thus, I show the best offer to that bank and I tell them I only consider to work with them if they beat that offer. I am not going to lie to you: there are banks which may not be willing to acquire new clients all the time, and so they will not make an effort to beat the offers from their competitors. Yet, this is absolutely worth the effort because many banks are receptive to improve their offers if you show them you have a better one from a competitor.

There are two important things to say about this process. The first thing is that you should always talk to the bank branch's manager. Speaking with a regular branch worker will not get you far, because most decisions are actually made by branch managers (especially if you are asking for special rates or terms). Plus, from my experience, the branch manager is the only person who really knows the realistic limits of the terms the bank can offer and he/she is the most motivated person in acquiring new clients to the bank (usually, they also get bonuses based on the number of new clients they acquire). The second thing I would like to mention is, if the bank is not willing to offer you better terms than the standard ones, then they are probably not a good business partner for you, because they may also not have flexibility to negotiate better rates later on (yes, you are right, my strategy also involves negotiating rates frequently).

Again, please note that the reality of banks, lenders and financial institutions is very different across different countries and therefore you must adapt this information to your own reality.

If the bank with the second best offer does not show any flexibility, then move on the third best, forth and even the fifth – as long as we are talking about reasonable differences to the best offer: although everything is negotiable, do not expect a bank to cut his offer in half just because you had a better offer from a competitor…

If you cannot get better rates or terms, then go to the bank with the best offer and start negotiating with them. Over the years, I found out that these arguments are especially fruitful during a negotiation:

1. "There is a realistic chance I become client and I am actually willing to have my income deposited on the new account that I will open at this bank". Usually banks are interested that you have your salary (and other income) deposited with them, because that increases their business volume and shows commitment (which is relevant for them in the long haul).

2. "I am starting to invest in real estate and I will be a long term client, who will ask for several loans". I found out that showing a future financial plan helped a lot, especially one with realistic yet appealing projections, showing that we are deep into real estate and we will acquire several properties in the future. Again, this works best if negotiated directly with the branch manager.

3. "I am considering to purchase other of your products and invest with you, either now or in the future", especially if you are looking for ways to diversify beyond real estate. There are some products and services provided by banks that may be of high interest to you, including investment non-taxable accounts and savings- and 401k-alike accounts. Important note: you should never ever lie during a negotiation (or in any other context, for that matter), so you should only use these arguments if you are in fact willing to apply them.

Once you have successfully negotiated better rates, you should get a pre-approval before actually going for shopping real estate, if you intend to finance the deal. A pre-approval will tell you how much you can spend on a new property (and also how much you have to put down for the deal to go through – a down payment is the amount of money you need to put in a deal so that a lender finances you). Also, in some countries real estate agents require that you are pre-approved in order to work with you.

How banks decide on loan eligibility

This was one of the book's hardest sections to write, because this is highly dependent on the context. First off, I want you to realize that the financial and the banking systems vary (a lot) among countries. In some countries, banks look at clients in a similar way, as far as creditworthiness is concerned, because there is a centralized credit score, like in the US, which both the person and the banks know. In other countries, each bank determines each client's "credit score" based on his/her personal history with the bank. Important credit information (such as previous defaults and the amount of debt each person has) is kept by a centralized entity, which provides it to lenders and clients (note that there is no concept of "score"). In some countries, banks are pretty much the only institutions to lend money for people to buy real estate, whether in other countries there are specialized lenders and mortgage-specialized banks (e.g. in the US known as thrift banks). Having that in mind, you must adapt the following information to your own reality.

This said, over the years I realized that there are a few factors that tend to be looked at by all banks, when it comes to loan eligibility:

1. *Credit score.* Just like I said, in some countries this is provided by a centralized entity or credit reporting agencies (such as Experian, TransUnion and Equifax in the US and Equifax Canada and TransUnion Canada in Canada). In other countries, each bank decides on each client's score individually.

2. *(previous) Relationship with lenders*. Because this is a very broad topic, I wrote the next section – "Relationships with banks and lenders" - to cover this in detail. It elaborates on the relationship with bank, branch and account managers, which I briefly mentioned before.

3. *Current income, types of income, debt ratios and employment status*. The section "Sell yourself to a bank" – two sections above - covers this part.

4. *Amount of loan, repayment history* and other factors. Lenders also consider how much they are lending you and what you want to do with the money. Usually, primary, owner occupied properties have better rates than second homes, but if you intend to rent the out, this usually plays to your favor. Also, if you have unpaid loans on which you defaulted this can seriously hinder your creditworthiness, so I always recommend to negotiate feasible payment plans on unpaid loans.

Relationships with banks and lenders

I have already talked about creating history with banks. In most countries, it is common to build credit history just for the sake of improving your history/score, as I said before. However, the relationship with a bank does not end there...

The first step towards a good relationship with a bank starts with an excellent relationship with your account manager first, and then the branch manager. Banks and lenders are institutions ran by people, so it all comes down to people and the relationship you have with them. Although banks are highly supported by software, which helps determining things like creditworthiness, as I said before, managers can always overwrite their software's guidelines and decisions, because software can only take into account a fraction of reality.

In fact, the bank representatives are those who ultimately take the most important decisions at banks. This is why you want to have a very solid relationship with the bank representatives you deal with: they will be the ones understanding your credibility and plans. Most investors, when they start investing in real estate, do not take this into account. They presume most bank representatives are simply vehicles between the bank and the clients. Nothing could be more wrong.

I suggest you develop a relationship with people. Talk to your account and your branch's managers. Show them you are savvy about the market and you have an investment plan that is solid and well thought out. In no time, they will be interested in you, because they will take you as a serious individual who wants to invest (a perfect client profile for a bank), and thus they will want to work with you. Working with means they will work to optimize your relationship with the bank, which will favor the bank and yourself.

Here are some suggestions so you improve your relationship with banks:

1. ***Create history.*** As I said, this is a great way to start a financial relationship with a financial institution, such as banks. But this is also an excellent way to start a personal relationship with a bank. You will

often be at the bank, talking with the representatives and thus developing a relationship with them. In the client's history, lenders also take into account how you have been a client and what your account size has been.

2. Have a look at possible financial products the bank has to offer which may be interesting to you, so you *increase your involvement with the bank*. This will improve your history before the bank. My first recommendation goes to saving-, investing- and retirement-alike accounts, which are usually attractive from a tax standpoint. This should also be carefully discussed with your accountant, who can advise you about tax implications. There are also credit cards that have very interesting benefits (especially to real estate investors who work with capital-intensive projects, like property remodels), such as payback and cash-advance.

3. *Share your plans with your account manager and the branch manager*. Perhaps you can even invite them to lunch – in some cultures this is acceptable/recommended, while in others it is not. Either way, it is important to show them how trustworthy you are, how savvy about real estate you are and what are your plans to invest as time goes by – thus showing them you will need to work with them on a consistent basis.

Sell yourself to a bank

This is the last (but not least) point in the context of negotiating with lenders. There are two different parts in a possible loan negotiation with lenders: loan eligibility, which determines whether you are eligible for a loan, and loan rates, which, if you qualify for a loan, are based on your financial situation and a few other things.

Showing a bank you have a solid financial situation is one of the best arguments you can have during a negotiation. Personally, I follow the exact same method when I want to finance a real estate deal: I make a report which shows my entire financial situation, and shows my real estate portfolio as a growing business (if you are interested in a template for this send an email to geral@arrowplus.pt). The report also shows the bank what they want to know. As I said, lenders usually assess loan applications with two things in mind: a collateral that covers the amount of credit, for a given LTV, and the financial capability to cover the loan's financial plan.

Therefore, you should show the bank that you have the requirements necessary to take the loan, and your financial capability is so strong, you should have good rates on the loan (in the US, the best rate available is called prime rate). Usually, the collateral is the real estate property itself, and so you will only need to buy a property under market value (the next chapter is all about this). If you nail this, you now need to show the second part of the equation – a strong financial capability – which is a little bit more complicated.

From my experience, there are 5 financial indicators that banks look for in a client, when it comes to assessing financial capability for a given loan financial plan:

1. The first and most fundamental thing is that ***the client has predictable income and employment stability***. The most predictable form of income is to have employment stability, which is better proven by having a permanent, full-time position (this usually means that employers have to pay a considerable amount of money to fire employees). Of course that this is not absolutely necessary in order to have a loan (especially because permanent positions are far from being what they were), otherwise many of my company's clients would never had been financed. However, having a permanent, long-term, full-time position is an indicator that your income is predictable and you are less likely to become unemployed than if you had a term position.

2. The second is to have *passive income*, i.e. income that you do not have to work for. This is, for example, capital gains, stock dividends and income from bonds or fixed-income securities, rental income (of other rental properties you may have, among others. In theory, the more diversified your passive income is the better, but unless you are asking for a very big loan, lenders are not likely to do that kind of a fine-detail assessments.

3. The third is *owning assets (especially real estate) in general* – in particular high-worth assets and debt-free assets. Depending on the bank you consider, this may not be relevant unless you are providing these assets as collateral.

4. The forth is *having no debt* (especially bad debt). Put yourself in the lender shoes for a while: how should you decide on loan eligibility? Of course that if a client already has a lot of debt (regarding his/her assets), it is more likely that he/she will default on the new loan, than if he/she did not have any debt. In particular, the more debt you have for the same assets/equity, the more likely you will default on a new loan. The same logic can be applied to *liabilities and income*. In fact, lenders usually consider ratios (*debt-to-equity or DTE and liabilities-to-income LTI ratios*) instead of absolute values. After a credit score – if that applies to your reality - these rations are the most important thing you should focus on (ideally, you should keep your LTI below 30%-40%, depending on the country you live in). Note: although the concepts of debt and liabilities are often used with the same meaning, I define debt as the amount of money you owe and liabilities as the sum of money you need to pay e.g. monthly on your debt (also called debt payments/installments). This is probably not congruent with the most standard definitions in the US, where Debt-To-Income (DTI) is a

widely used term. Just so this is clear, DTI and LTI mean the same according to my definitions.

5. Finally, many banks value *ensured-returns*. Of course that there are not 100%-ensured returns, because in life nothing is 100% certain or ensured. But just like in 1. - predictable income – a long-term position suggests that you will maintain your income level, investments you make that are somehow ensured (by someone) suggest that you will continue to receive that money in future. For instance, turn-key properties whose rental income is ensured by a company (just like my company offers to its clients) is a good example of this.

Note that these are some of the aspects banks consider when deciding on credit eligibility, but some of them are not even required – they will simply help you qualifying for a loan and/or have better rates on that loan. My advice is pretty simple: if you have the possibility of having some of the indicators I mentioned above, then it is possible, according to my experience, to increase your odds of qualifying for a loan and have better rates on it.

Artur Mariano

7

Searching and negotiating properties

Real estate investing is all about "buying well", i.e. doing great deals when buying real estate. This can mean a lot of things, but essentially it means to buy real estate under the market value. The biggest the difference between what you pay and what the property is worth, the better succeeded, on average, each investment will be. The truth is that the best way to make money with real estate is to buy low (rather than selling high).

This is, therefore, a central topic of real estate investing. Searching for undervalued properties is a complex process and time-consuming. Therefore, I have dedicated this whole chapter to this topic, while I present you the method I use to search for properties under these premises. Plus, negotiating properties is a crucial factor to buy properties under the market value and so I also leave you a series of tips and techniques that you can use when negotiating real estate.

How to look for properties under market value

Assuming you have already determined how you will finance a deal (either all cash or leveraging – see Chapter 6 on how to negotiate with lenders), it is time to move onto actually buying real estate. As I said before, the best way to earn money with real estate is buying well, instead of hoping to sell real estate later on well above its market value.

Thus, it makes sense to invest most of your time into this: looking for undervalued properties. But the truth is that there are no magic formulas or big secrets; most of what I teach you in this chapter requires work and is time-consuming. As with everything in life, it is not possible to achieve a lot doing little. Same thing to buy well: you will need to invest some time into it and know the best ways to do it – it is that simple.

The importance of your relationship with real estate agents and being a "serious" buyer

The most standard way to find properties is through real estate companies. Therefore, it makes sense to base your strategy around good relationships with those companies and, better yet, real estate agents. In my opinion, real estate agents have the biggest impact in the entire real estate industry. They define and adjust listing prices, negotiate values (both up and down), promote properties, etc.

Having a good relationship with real estate agents is thus one of the best things an investor can do, if his/her intention is to invest in the long term. Personally, I have some friends who are real estate agents, and I also have a good relationship with real estate agents I met after I started to invest in real estate. When I started investing in real estate, I actually used a pretty bad strategy: I was distant and I simply told agents what I was looking for. The result could not have been worse: I was always offered bad-to-reasonable deals, at bad-to-reasonable prices. Nothing exciting, nothing close to what I was looking for – the best deals. One day I decided to invite a real estate for a coffee (inviting someone for a coffee is pretty common in my country), and I invested some time explaining him what I really wanted. And the best deals started to pop up...

I am not telling you that real estate agents will magically make great deals pop out of the blue. And I am not telling you a real estate agent will, all of a sudden, offer you the best deals ever because you invited him to have a coffee or lunch. The fundamental question is that, being upfront with agents and telling them exactly what you are looking for and why you are looking for those deals, will increase your odds of getting what you are looking for. First, because the agent knows exactly what you are looking for. Second, because he will take you as a serious buyer, i.e. someone who really wants to buy real estate (versus someone who is just curious about the topic).

Being a serious buyer has a lot of benefits. It would be illusory to think that there are not truly exceptional deals, which real estate agents (either occasionally or more often than occasionally) have access to. Bankruptcies, foreclosures that can be avoided, short sales, divorces or simply a really good listing price. Guess who the real estate agents will show these deals first, after putting them on their platforms? Any intelligent agent would first talk to the clients who are more likely to take these deals – and that is what they do. They know that giving these deals to their best clients will make the clients come for more, on and on... Being a frequent buyer – or a serious buyer, at thee are often referred to as – has hedges.

In short, real estate agents will not offer you the best deals because you invited them for a coffee or lunch. However, they will likely offer you deals closer to what you are looking for if you tell them what is that you are looking for, and why do you want those deals. Plus, the person supposed to see merit in those deals is you – not the agents – and that is why you need a good strategy (as I showed you in Chapter 3). If your strategy is based on finding properties under market value, you can increase your chances of getting a deal like that if you ask several agents to present you such deals when they pop up. Always talk and have good relationships with many agents in parallel.

A method to find properties

In my opinion, the best thing about real estate investing is the fact that we can negotiate properties at a much lower value than what they are actually work (see Chapter 1 where I compare real estate with other investments, such as the stock market). This is actually the reason why we can obtain very high yields in real estate: we can buy way undervalue; in my opinion, it is easier to buy properties under the market value than to rent them out above the market value.

As you probably realized while reading the earlier chapters of this book, the philosophy I use in my life is that, to be successful, we have to work hard to get it. For example, for me to obtain certain yield figures, even though my method works great for me, I must invest a lot of time into looking for properties. The alternative for early investors is to hire a specialized company, like mine, but you need to take their costs into account.

Therefore, if you have the time and the will, you could follow my method, which is not going to add any costs on top of what you pay for the property. I cannot assure you my method will bring you excellent results, because I cannot control your execution of it – and a ton of other variables – but I can tell you it has been working very well for me, for years, both when looking for real estate for my own and my company's clients. The method itself is in fact very simple:

1. First, I look for real estate that has been in the market for a while (the more, the better). This is because owners tend to be more receptive to

negotiating when their properties have been listed for a long time (and they have got very low-ball offers or no offers at all).

2. Second, I first get to know the actual market price of all properties I identified in 1., using comparative methods. This allows me to know what the properties I visit are actually worth, so I can make an offer with high confidence.

3. Third, I always determine the actual renovation costs by visiting prospective properties with a contractor I rely on. This is always a contractor I worked in the past, so that I already know him and how accurate he is when it comes to quotes. Moreover, I always do this before actually submitting an offer (see more on remodels in Chapter 8).

4. Lastly, I submit an offer that allows me to buy under market value and reflects the yield rate I want to get. In this phase, I do not look into the listing price anymore; I know how much the property will rent out for, I know how much I will spend on renovation and I know what is the yield I want to obtain at the end, so it becomes very simple math. Hint: a lot (and I mean a lot) of my offers are rejected immediately.

This method may seem very simple, but the truth is that is has been working quite well for me. Now, the probability you find a property whose owner is willing to sell it in similar terms to these is actually quite low… so this method also assumes that you submit several different offers in parallel! In general, one offer is not enough to get a good deal. Personally, I submit 10-20 offers for every property I actually acquire.

But let us come back to the beauty of real estate: even if a given property is listed for $500.000, no one will prevent you from submitting a much lower offer, such as $150.000. There is nobody preventing the owner from accepting it either. Do understand, however, that only a very small set of homeowners would consider an offer like this, because your offer would simply be too far off the asking price.

However, even if only 1% of owners are willing to accept such an offer (for any possible reason) we are assuming, statistically speaking, that 1 out of every 100 offers will be accepted. Is all your effort (in visiting and analyzing 100 properties and submitting 100 offers) worth it, we could ask?

If this method sounds weird, unusual or even complicated, you may actually be right. In fact, only a small fraction of investors submit several offers in parallel and very few actually search for properties in a similar way to my method...

According to this method, more than one of your offers may actually be accepted. Remember, however, that you must submit conditional offers (for instance, the offer only becomes valid if you can get the deal financed or you have no other offers accepted – talk to your real estate agent and explain him the situation). There are several legal ways to avoid becoming bounded to an offer, as long as you think about it before submitting it (once it is live, you gave your word, and so you should never try to walk away from the deal). But if you are making tons of concurrent offers which result in great yields (or acquisitions well above market value), you should actually consider taking all offers that are accepted (even if it takes looking for extra financing), unless you really cannot take them.

The last step of my method has to do with offers that are actually considered but you get a counter. From my experience, when there are counters to very low-ball offers, then there is a real interest to sell. Therefore, we find ourselves in a favorable situation. What I usually do in cases like this is to submit and offer that realistically devalues the property, i.e. an offer that realistically reports all the bad aspects about the property. This means, I come up with a list of arguments that devalue the property, based on the renovation that is to be done, the location, and a few other factors.

I usually do not look at – and I believe you should do the same – to this final step as "for me to win, somebody has to lose". First, you buying a property under market value does not mean someone will lose. Imagine this reason, which is one among many possibilities: the seller found another deal or opportunity where he/she will double his/her money in a very short time. Even by selling a property under its market value, he/she will end up winning with the transaction.

There are a lot more reasons why the seller may not lose, though. Imagine the seller had already bought the property way under market value, and will make a profit even by selling again under the market value. Or imagine the seller wants to buy another property – a great deal – and does not want to lose that deal. Or imagine the sellers sees his/her property as a problem, not as an asset (for instance, they cannot rent it out and they incur expenses, such as taxes and maintenance, every quarter). As you see, all these reasons show that a seller can still make a profit or be in a better position after selling a property under the market value.

Other sources of properties

Of course that real estate companies are not the only alternatives, when it comes to looking for properties. Other than real estate companies, you can look for properties directly with the owners, actions, short sales and liquidations of assets as a result of a bankruptcy, etc. As an individual, when I start investing in real estate, I stared where most investors start at: online listings and real estate agents. However, as the investor becomes savvier, he/she can start tapping into other sources of properties (where usually there are better deals but more risk and bureaucracy involved). Today, when I want to buy more properties, I simply use my company's structure to look for them, as any real estate investment company would do (depending on where you live and the license you have, it may not be allowed to use a license to buy or sell real estate for yourself). For that reason, today I can access great deals through my company, but this was not the case all along. These are the other sources of properties that I have explored successfully over the years:

1. *Auctions*. Depending on where you live, auctions can be a great place to find deals, although there are some downsides to them. First off, depending on the country you live in, auctions usually apply to

foreclosures and tax deed sales, although there may be others. The (mortgage) foreclosure auction happens when the borrower defaults on his/her mortgage, they go through an entire legal process and the property eventually makes it to an auction. A tax deed sale (also called tax foreclosure) is a result of a property owner failing to pay his/her property taxes, even after several notifications. The main question that every investor should ask is why did any property actually made it to an action; if the property was good enough, maybe a family member of the debtor would have paid for it? Or the previous owner would have made more to retain his/her property? Well, many homes that make it to auctions have problems (mostly title issues) such as having liens on them. A particularly interesting scenario though, is when properties make it to auctions because they were inherited and there is no heir that has the money (or the interest) to buy the property from the other heirs.

The most important thing about auctions, however, is *timing*. Because they happen very quickly, the entire auction procedure is usually carried out on a very short notice (my experience tells me this is the case for most types of auctions). This has two important aspects to it: first, sometimes it is actually impossible to actually visit the property before the auction. But make no mistake: there are tons of people willing to buy properties without visiting them. Secondly, buyers at auctions must have the capital to buy the properties. There is no "I will auction this property and get a mortgage afterwards". This is important because it creates an entrance barrier and creates some pressure on the buyers.

2. ***Foreclosures***. I know talk about foreclosures that remain with the bank (i.e. have not gone on auction). Typically, there is a slight discount on foreclosured properties. From my experience, it is extremely hard to get very good deals consistently through foreclosures, because banks are

tightly connected to the real estate market (this may or may not be the case in your country). In many systems, banks tend to be greedy players; plus, in some countries they are so tightly connected to the real estate market (e.g. their business is based on the housing markets, through mortgage loans) that they have no interest that the overall price of real estate goes down. History has shown us that, in some cases, banks kept foreclosures (and even pulled some off the market on purpose) so that the housing market did not go down. Also, keep in mind that foreclosures can come at a discount but they can also come with a myriad of problems. Unlike deals that go through real estate companies, usually banks take no responsibility with problems in foreclosured homes. From my experience, it is not possible to negotiate with banks based on the problems foreclosured homes have, or negotiate at all sometimes! Banks are typically not flexible regarding commissions, payment, etc... We can forget all those out-of-the-box strategies to buy homes, such as seller financed deals, split payments, etc. So have all this into account (and do your own research in the area you live in) when considering foreclosured homes as a source of deals.

3. **Bankruptcies.** Although this type of properties may eventually get to auctions, that does not always happen. As for bankruptcies, the investor can look for deals directly with companies that are about to file for bankruptcy. These are companies that may, depending on the circumstances, be willing to negotiate their assets at a much lower price, so they can possibly survive or keep themselves afloat for longer. They do not regard their assets as valuable assets because, truth be told, they will not be worth anything if they cannot avoid bankruptcy. Of course that finding companies that are in this position does not come for free. It is usually necessary to do a lot of research and/or get along with businessmen and tell them you are looking for these companies; people

in the industry will know better than anyone what is going on with their partners and competitors.

Negotiating properties with success

As I said before, you should never feel guilty or think that you are taking advantage of the owners you are buying properties from, when you are negotiating (I assume you will not actually take advantage of any situation, such as you knowing the seller will sell at any price to pay for e.g. medical bills and based on that submitting really low offers – please never do something like that! It is possible to negotiate properties successfully with full integrity). This being said, you should look at this as a negotiation where potential buyers submit their best offers based on the yield they want to achieve and buyers will accept the offers that, somehow, will meet their expectations and interests. In particular, sellers can actually accept below-market offers and still do a great deal (as I showed you before).

In a property negotiation, the sides (whether they are represented by agents or not) will try to lower and increase the asking price and the offer, respectively. There is, however, a series of arguments that I often resort to during the negotiation of a given property. Let me introduce them to you…

Too big of a remodel…

The property needs a "huge make over". As you can see, I leave things up in the air. What is a "huge make over"? That is actually a very relative term, but whoever may hear it will think "big costs" immediately. More often than not, this is actually true, because we can do a remodel as big (and expensive) as we want. In particular, there are a few "special" arguments you can use, if they are true:

1. ***The roof.*** Depending on the reality in your country, if the roof needs to be redone, that can be the most expensive part of the remodel. Roofs and roof materials can be expensive in some countries. In Portugal,

where I come from, roofs are expensive because they require a lot of manpower and they are made with ceramic tile, an expensive material. In the United States, roof shingles are the most common roofing material. Roof shingles usually deteriorate faster but they are also cheaper.

2. ***The facade***. Again, this may be a very expensive part of remodeling a property, depending on variables such as where you live and the legislation therein. In Portugal – a very old country – city councils and tend to control facade remodeling to a fine detail, which can increase costs and, to a larger extent, time to execution. In the US, it is usually the homeowners association in the neighborhood or city can also control the remodeling of facades and limit homeowners to a set of colors they can use on their property's facade.

3. ***The electrical and the plumbing systems***. If we need to gutter and redo the entire property, we should often redo the electrical and the plumbing as well. This is usually because guttering the property requires a lot of work and money, and so it often makes sense to invest some extra capital and redo the electrical and the plumbing. If the investor will not gutter the property, these systems can mean a very high cost both in labor and materials, and is thus a perfect argument to use, if we plan on redoing them.

Too much bureaucracy

The fact there is a lot of bureaucracy and paper work – which has costs – associated with any remodeling. From my experience, the bureaucracy in the markets I operate (especially that that pertains to city council regulation) has been increasing over the last years. In fact, if you talk to developers who were mainly active in the 80s and 90s, they will tell you that before, construction was way simpler and less regulated. Given that the majority of people is afraid of the paperwork associated with property renovation, they will likely see merit in this argument and agree that the entire process is a hassle, thus potentially becoming more flexible in the negotiation.

Location

It is very hard to conclude that a given location is the best one, because that is a very dubious question. Therefore, it is easy to use the location as an argument during a negotiation, by simply saying that "the location is not the best possible". However, it is also easy for the seller to counter with "it is not the worst either". Thus, the location of the property (one of the most important factors in real estate investing) is really something that you should focus on and talk about during a negotiation (unless it is in fact a prime location – in that case you probably do not want to discuss that subject at all, if you are buying).

In short, I am obviously not telling you to take advantage of anyone or any situation. I am simply giving you better arguments when it comes to negotiating real estate. Never, ever cross the line of law and ethics. From my experience, it is possible to make unbelievable deals (sometimes for both ends) and a lot of money with a very ethical negotiation process, let alone a legal one. Never lie and never omit important details of the property if you are selling it – but do not talk about the pluses of a property if you are buying it.

In alternative to negotiating a property by yourself (since negotiating may not be right up your alley – and you should be able to realize that) you can, as I also suggest for other things, hire a specialized company to do the job for you. In some countries, it is actually common to hire real estate agents to negotiate the property on behalf of buyers. This may or may not be the reality in your own country; either way, keep in mind that even if you think of yourself as a good negotiator, agents and companies may know the market better and they will have more experience in negotiating and trading real estate.

Artur Mariano

8

Renovation works

Most of the properties that are suited for investing need to be renovated. However, if you want to buy properties way under value, you will probably have to target properties that need to be completely redone, as these properties are usually devalued by the owners themselves and the market. Renovation of properties is thus a fundamental side of real estate investing, and thus this chapter.

The key aspects about property renovation

In my view, the renovation of properties has two key aspects: the people who will execute the renovation (the contractor, the engineers/architects, etc) and the materials that are needed for the renovation. Obviously, there are a lot of other important factors, such as the necessity of a project to carry out the renovation – depending on its extent – the legal bureaucracy attached to the renovation, etc. However, this depends on your own country's reality, and I believe that 90% of a successful renovation comes down to the people and the materials, so I will cover those two aspects in this chapter.

Developers and contractors

If you never remodeled a property, you do not know yet that human labor is, much more often than not, the most expensive part of the renovation. Therefore, finding good, serious contractors, who have market or below-market rates, is crucial. Today, I work with contractors who I rely 100% on, and whom I hire without the need for supervision, given that I have been working with them for a long time now. However, finding trustworthy and reliable contractors with reasonable rates and one can hire without supervision can be a very complicated task, especially for rookie investors.

Here is what you can do to maximize the chances of finding such contractors:

1. *Ask for references*. Talk to other investors, who already remodeled several properties. This is the easiest way to collect good references – ask for someone honest, serious and reliable. Ideally, you should see renovations that were executed by such people before hiring them. Also, ask for references regarding post-renovation warranty, how easy they are to get a hold of once the bill has been paid for, whether they can meet deadlines, etc.

2. *Be honest and upfront with the contractor you end up hiring*. From my experience, it is crucial to be honest and upfront with contractors before the renovation agreement is actually signed. Setbacks are possible in any renovation, because you can only inspect the property fully after you actually bought it and started the renovation. While you may be entitled a property inspection before closing a deal, in many systems owners do not expect that you damage the property just so you can check whether there is damage (the foundation, plumbing, etc being

the most important areas). However, some contractors may take advantage of this and other situations – there are honest and dishonest professionals in every sector. As such, always be honest and upfront with contractors – and find trustworthy contractors who you can rely on. They will be some of your best strategic partners in your real estate investing career.

3. ***Put all the terms of the renovation on paper.*** This is a mistake I have seen countess times: any renovation – big or small - that you agree on must be put on paper, through a carefully prepared contract. From my experience, I can tell you that it is very common, when there is no written contract, that people have different opinions regarding what was agreed on. And that is actually expected. I myself forget about things I said or I think I said. And probably so do you, especially if your life is as shaky and busy as mine. The same may happen to contractors. Thus, always put the terms of the renovation on paper and include as much detail as possible (e.g. I often talk about specific tiling position, wall angles, etc if I feel that is important).

4. ***Overview the renovation***. There is nothing better than supervising the renovation either by yourself (if you have the time) or by hiring a company or some person to do it for yourself. This is relevant because 1) you will have the chance to correct any mistakes in real estate - as you seen them – 2) you will know how everything is done (which is relevant for the future) and 3) you have the opportunity to control the renovation to a fine detail. I will also leave you an important tip: take photographs from the renovation as often as possible, they will be very relevant in the future (e.g. allow you to track the progress, see what is inside the walls, etc).

Materials

In my opinion, investors should choose the materials for renovating properties based on how much money they can make on them. In other words, think about it this way: can you increase the rent of the property, once the renovation is done, if you choose a $40 per square meter tile, other than another one that costs $8 per square meter? When it comes to renovation materials, you can literally go with anything from feast to famine.

My general recommendation is that you limit your rehab budget to the rent you expect to collect on a given property. Remember the method to look for properties? At this point, before actually buying the property, you should already know how much you can spend in the rehab. At this point, you should only shrink it, and not stretch it, based on the rent you expect to collect. However, keep in mind that, generally speaking, the renovation materials do not make a huge difference in the final rent you can get on a property. In fact, rent is mostly defined by the location and the type of property, including how many bedrooms it has, whether it has a pool or not, etc. The materials (both look- and quality-wise) are primarily and indicator for how fast you can rent out a property, as it will look more or less attractive to prospective tenants.

At the same time, the price of the materials is not necessarily reflected on the quality of the remodel, as well as the rent. However, there is a certain standard that is expected, as far as the quality of the materials, for a given property at a given location. Therefore, there is a minimum standard you need to abide by. If you are in the luxury segment, you cannot use low-tier materials, for instance. I usually select the quality of the materials based on the type of property and kind of tenants I expect to have in the properties. For example, when the properties are rented out to families, they should have different materials than when tenants are students. I am not suggesting students deserve less comfort or quality than a family. However, they do have different requirements and therefore you should go with different materials. At the same time, different target audiences will appreciate and value different things. For instance, a family will probably appreciate a stone countertop that is especially pretty, while students may prefer a barbecue area where they can party. You know your target audience better than me (if not, I suggest you do your research on it), so you will have to be the judge of that.

My overall point is that, although you do have to keep up with the standards required for a given property, you need to choose the renovation materials that increase the yield of the deal, while maintaining a given level of sophistication and comfort in the property. At the same time, choosing cheaper materials can still result in an excellent remodeling. You will have to use common sense and adjust to your target audience.

I was lucky enough to stay at several hotels, in the entire world, from 3- to 5-star hotels. In some 5-star hotels I had the impression that the materials were not as pretty as in some 4- or 3-star hotels. Taste and price are not necessarily connected. My advice is to either look at interior design magazines to grab some ideas, or hire someone for the job. I always try to cut down on costs like this, so I came up with a few tiling combinations that I tested before, and now I simply stick to those because I know they will come out really nice. There is also an important tip I usually give out to clients: there are several things that improve the looks of a home and do not increase the costs of the renovation. For example, several 5-star hotels I stayed at were really nicely remodeled, and eventually I found some patterns in these renovations; more than the materials themselves, it was the form how the materials were used that made a difference. The form you apply tiles and play with them has nothing to do with their price.

At the same time, if you have good relationships with retail managers in the construction sector (companies like Home Depot in the US or Leroy Merlin and Bauhaus in Europe – I am not affiliated with any of these companies), always ask for opinions on the material you buy. They are the experts in the subject, as they deal with complains all the time. They know what brands are usually returned and what brands usually have no problems. As for tiling materials, there are a lot of top brands that sell refurbished tiles, which are usually defect somehow (not caught by the human eye, most of the time) and way cheaper. I usually select this type of tile to work with and because I work with the medium sector – thus never going with the higher-end material - I barely notice any difference in the looks of the homes (only in the looks of my pockets…).

In short, you should think about the yield of the property when you choose the rehab materials. You should also follow a given standard, based on the type and location of the property (and the target audience). You can follow or even copy what is pretty – do not go with your personal taste, prefer what works best for the average person because you will not live in the investment properties either way. Ask for opinions and follow magazines for professionals or hotels, if you can.

Other aspects of renovations

Of course that limiting renovations to labor and materials is a very simplistic approach, which ignores several other very important points about renovations.

For instance, as I said before, the foundation and the façade of a building (or house, for that matter) should be carefully inspected before you actually buy the property and start renovation. For instance, if the foundation is made out of wood (and not concrete – which is vastly more common in Europe), you need to make sure the foundation is rock solid before actually proceeding with the rest of the renovation. This is a very important point because there is usually a big difference, legislation-wise, between a renovation that includes modifying the foundation and one that does not. This is because foundations have typically to be assessed by engineers and/or architects. Please check the legislation in your own country on house renovations, because they are way too different from country to country. In some European countries I have studied in this regard, changing or fixing the foundation of the building/property requires a project done by an engineer and/or an architect, and needs to be validated by a regulator (usually the city council or an equivalent institution). We all know that these institutions get clogged up with work very easily, and so these processes tend to be lengthy. So, in general, changing or fixing a foundation comes at two costs: 1) it is more expensive because you need to get more people involved and potentially pay for an engineering project and 2) they take way longer because this process has to be validated (and often supervised) by a regulator. For these reasons, if the legislation in your country is not permissive, then you are probably better-off looking for properties that do not need fixes in the foundation.

Another important point about renovations is the state of the plumbing and the electrical system of the property. It is extremely important to inspect the status of these systems before you buy a property, to determine whether they need to be replaced. Sometimes it is actually hard to determine this before buying a property, because damage has to be done. However, when starting a renovation, make sure to always check the plumbing because it is actually easy to replace the system if you gutter the house anyways, but extremely hard if you try to do it afterwards (i.e. once the renovation is done). Also, I almost always replace the plumbing system of the entire house when renovating it, because if you do the math, it should come out at more than 10% of the entire renovation, so it makes sense to put up a bit more and actually get the entire system new.

Another very important questions is following the budget defined at the beginning of the renovation. When we start a renovation, there is a lot of excitement, because transforming real estate is a beautiful process. Everything looks organized and ready to go, because after all, we have got a plan! But the truth of the matter is that, if you do not follow the renovation closely since day 1, it is actually very easy for things to go south and you lose control. Among other things, contractors start to buy "little things" that "were not expensive enough for them to bother you". It is possible that they run short on materials, or they need to return some. It is possible they do not show up, or they charge for time they have not worked (unless you are there – or have someone to be there, you will not know!), etc. This is why I always recommend to have a specialized company overseeing the renovation to make sure everything runs smoothly, should you not be able to be there. This costs money, yes, but it may save you a ton over the long run.

9

Rent out/ sell your real estate

Although it is true that "buying well" is the biggest "secret" of the entire real estate investing game, it is also true that if you do not rent out (for buy and hold) or sell (for fix and flip), buying way undervalue will not do much for you. Rent out or sell your real estate properties is an absolutely crucial step, which just like any of the other steps, has a lot of room for optimization.

In this chapter, I will give you several tips to optimize these two processes, based on my experience, which I acquired throughout the years.

Leasing contracts

The vast majority of people I asked why they are not willing to give real estate a shot, they always answer "problems with tenants" as the main reason. It seems that everyone has a cousin or an uncle who actually did "the real estate thing" and it seem that all of them ended up having all kinds of "horror stories involving tenants". I think that the majority of people who think this way belong to an older generation, and I think that most young people are way more keen on investing in real estate. In fact, in my country, the rental market today has nothing to do with the rental market 20, 10 or even 5 years ago. We can definitely start seeing a shift in people's mentality, towards renting and owning to rent.

Today, the rental market in Portugal is more solid and has less bad procedures that were standard back in the day. Tenants are now prepared to have co-signers (see below) and they know what are their duties. In your country, applying for a rental may be a standard thing for more than 20 years. If you ask a Portuguese person whether they want to "apply for a rental property", they will laugh the hell out of you. Well, this is changing over time, and as the society increasingly understands the upside of renting versus owning, things like this may be more and more accepted. Maybe you live in a country where getting to know tenants income is just as hard as in Portugal: many people will tell you "how much I make is none of your business". Or maybe not. Maybe you come from a country, such as those in northern Europe, where tenants see the landlord as an authority, someone who deserves respect, credit and has to be pleased. OK, perhaps this is not true across all northern European countries, but it was the reality in the northern European country I lived in.

Regardless where you live and what the reality of your country is, when it comes to the rental market, I think that there is a list of things that can only improve your leasing contracts and protect you as a landlord (as long as they are legal in your area). You can always start with a sample lease agreement – an outline to create your lease – and improve from there. Countries (and states) may have a tenant- or a landlord-friendly law, and they are so different from one another that some things are perfectly legal in some countries while absolutely illegal in others. The following tips I am sharing with you are my best tips to improve leases, based on what is legal in the markets I operate in. Always remember to have an attorney look into any lease you ultimately sign and settle.

1. Get *co-signers* on the leasing contract. In my country, this is finally becoming an accepted practice. I cannot know whether this is acceptable in your country, but if you can, including this in a leasing contract may become the ultimate form of insurance. Co-signers are people who also sign the leasing contract and they become responsible (if it is defined that way – always check the legislation in your country) for all the duties of the contract, the payment of which being the main one. When prospective tenants tell me they do not want to include co-signers, I simply do not rent out my homes. My perspective is that any tenant who expects to pay the rent on time and intends to cause no damage to the home should have no problem in having co-signers; therefore, it they deny having them, that tells me they may actually be not good tenants or they do not intend to follow the contract. As such, I do not rent them any of my homes – as simple as that.

2. *Minimum periods for early lease terminations.* It is usually better for both the tenant and the landlord – but mostly for the landlord – that there is a minimum time period to communicate an early lease termination. As a landlord, you want to minimize vacancies and therefore the bigger this time span is, the better you can plan and position your property in the market. Thus, try to make these periods as long as you can! In some countries, these periods may be standardized and not flexible. In other countries, contracts may be completely changed as long as both the tenant and the landlord agree on the specified terms.

3. *Landlord and, especially, tenant responsibilities.* As a landlord, you must defend your position, but you should never take advantage of anyone. Contracts should be legal, correct and... fair. This being said,

you should try to spell out as many tenant responsibilities as possible. Things like maintenance inside and outside the property, removal of trash and snow, landscaping, etc. When everything goes well, everything goes well. But whenever things go south, both sides start digging into the lease agreement to find out who is right. And that is when you realize that you should have detailed some terms with some finer detail. For example, if you do not specify who is cleaning out the property (especially at the end), tenants may walk away from it without doing much cleaning. You see, telling whether a home is cleaned or not is a very subjective question. Tenants are supposed to deliver the property to the landlord in about the same condition to which it was delivered, taking into account ordinary wear and tear. But this is different from how cleaned the property is. From my experience, the only way to ensure that the property is cleaned at the end of the lease is to include a term that forces professional cleaning at the end. This term alone has saved me thousands of bucks throughout my career as a landlord.

4. Pay attention to *the furniture in the property*. The leasing contract should list all furniture in the property, as well as its state. I typically ask my property manager to take photographs of the property and the furniture, and tenants sign the photos together with the leasing contract before actually entering the property. I have also seen many experienced landlords going inside the property with an action camera and record the entire visit, while commenting on the state of both the property and the furniture. Ideally, this video is then sent per email and tenants confirm that the furniture is in the same condition as it is in the video, when the lease starts.

5. ***Record the property condition when the lease starts***. Similarly to the furniture, I have seen many landlords recording the property itself with

an action camera, while making comments on its condition. Again, the video should be sent per email and its validity confirmed by the tenants before the lease actually starts. Just in case, like I said, I also ask my property manager to take photos of the property and have tenants sign them. The best thing to do is to attach the photos to the leasing contract and write a term that states something like "the condition of the property is recorded through photos, which are attached to this lease", which the tenants confirm and sign.

6. *Property condition when tenants leave*. Leases should, in my opinion, clearly state that the property should be delivered in the same condition it was received, except for ordinary wear and tear.

7. *Returning the security deposit*. I follow the German method when it comes to returning the security deposit. In some countries, it is actually common to use the security deposit as the last rent of the contract. Nothing could be more wrong! I always agree with my tenants that I will deliver them (it is actually my property manager doing it) the security deposit up to 5 days after the property keys are returned. This gives me the opportunity to return the security deposit safely, i.e. after I know the property is in fact in good condition.

Remember to have all leases done or checked by an attorney. You are probably not a law expert and lease templates are far from being bullet-proof. In fact, most lease templates out there will state the obvious, but not tips like these, which are what really makes the difference at the end.

Relationship with tenants

In my opinion, it is best to have a flexible relationship with tenants, i.e. trying to create as much value as possible for tenants and be there every time they need. For instance, responding quickly to maintenance (or any other) requests is crucial. At the same time, I learned that it is necessary to keep a certain distance to tenants. In particular, I learned that having a very close relationship with tenants can have many disadvantages. In short, do not give your tenants any reasons to complain about you, or want to leave your properties, but do not let them enter your personal life. See your tenants as clients: you should have an excellent commercial relationship, but not a personal one.

Show yourself available to help your tenants in everything you can, though. There are several things that you, as a landlord, can help. Reference letters and documents attesting the situation of tenants (especially students and foreigners) are good examples of things landlords can help with. At the same time, it is important that you respond to all maintenance requests as fast and as efficiently as possible. This is probably the most important thing for the majority of tenants (and the easiest way for tenants to assess landlords there is), in my opinion.

As for the communication you maintain with tenants, I recommend that you keep all correspondence by e-mail or any other traceable method (e.g. registered mail). It is quite likely that tenants will contact you through other channels, such as via phone calls or social networks – if you accept them as friends – as that is more convenient, however you should reject this as much as possible. It is way simpler to prove communication, agreements and settlements if you can refer back to registered communication. Otherwise - believe me - there will a lot of misunderstandings regarding what was actually agreed upon. Lastly, I recommend to have your attorney (or team – see this topic further in the book) know about the communication you maintain with tenants whenever it makes sense (which is actually more often than what people think).

Regarding insurance, what is common in my market, is that each person insures his/her belongings. For instance, for tenants to have their assets insured, they should buy their own insurance (unless it is agreed otherwise, of course). However, you as landlord should also have insurance for any damage you cause – through your real estate – to your tenants or any other people, for that matter. For instance, imagine that, due to bad weather, your roof breaks loose, hitting someone or someone's assets. My best recommendation is for you to talk to an insurance broker about all these scenarios and what kind of insurance makes sense for your personal case, based on what real estate you have and where you live.

Commissions and other costs

If you follow a "buy and hold" strategy, and you actually look at your portfolio as a long term project, my suggestion is to "set up a very functional machine", if you will. Sadly, commissions, fees and costs associated to maintenance, promotion of units and increasing the portfolio are simply too high. Thus, in order to keep your margins at a level where you can actually set up a business out of your portfolio, you will have to, sooner or later, have a very solid logistic platform of yours. Such a "platform" should include, in my opinion:

1. *Legal counseling*. Whatever is the size of the portfolio you already have or expect to build, I highly recommend to have a privileged connection to a lawyer or attorney (in some countries, there are other figures that can give legal counseling, so you need to check that for your own country). There will be a lot of legal questions associated to such a portfolio, and it will be necessary to often clear up questions regarding leases, the relationship with tenants, etc. Usually, you can agree on a monthly subscription with an attorney, based on an expected amount of work, which is directly correlated with the size of your portfolio. My best advice is not to cut on costs when it comes to legal matters.

2. *Maintenance*. For some portfolios, it makes sense to hire a property manager just to manage your own portfolio. In some places, this person can be called "super" (this term can also be used for the person who maintains a condominium). Consider the volume of your portfolio and

the kind of income it brings in, when assessing the possibility of hiring your own super.

3. ***Promoting your real estate***. Promoting your real estate is absolutely crucial to have success in a buy and hold portfolio. Of course that you can hire a real estate company or agent to do this for you, but their commissions may be way too high in some cases. Thus, it is advisable that you have your own promotion channels, including in social media or even your own website, if your portfolio is big enough.

4. ***Cleaning your properties***. Since I started my investments, I located and worked with professional cleaning companies, which ensure that properties are cleaned whenever it is necessary. This also allows me to recommend a trustworthy company to my tenants, whenever they leave the property and do not want to clean it up themselves (or do a bad job on that). At the same time, I am very confident about the final result because I already know their services.

5. ***Good relationships with store managers***. As I have mentioned before, having good relationships with the "players" of the real estate market you are in will be very beneficial over the long term. With "good relationships", I mean close relationships, by becoming a partner with those people and entities, and show them that you trust them to carry out and scale your business. Although you should not expect for exceptional conditions – you should not develop relationships having that in mind anyways – but keep in mind that all systems are made out and made by people, so at the end of the day it is people who actually come up with solutions.

6. ***Sponsorships***. If you do big renovation works, that actually grab some attention, you can actually obtain a sponsorship. The best way to do that is showing potential sponsors that you have interesting (meaning popular) channels where you can promote your real estate and

renovation works, such as a website, a blog or big social network followings. After that, you simply have to capitalize on the good relationships that you have with construction store managers.

Sell your real estate

If you follow the "fix and flip" strategy, you should consider a very different structure than what you would need, should you follow a "buy and hold" strategy. For instance, there will be no relationship with tenants, there is no maintenance (unless right after you sell the property, if that is agreed upon).

With a "fix and flip" strategy, there are, however, several other different things to consider. This strategy is based on buying real estate, renovate it and sell it. Therefore, there are several optimizations you can do, namely:

1. ***Have (even) more developers to work with***. If the "renovation works" is a big factor in the "buy and hold" strategy, it is even more important in the "fix and flip" strategy. This is probably where there is more room for optimization, together with finding good properties.

2. ***Lower commissions by selling directly to the costumers***. If you can sell your real estate directly to buyers, then you can save tons of money on commissions that you would otherwise pay to real estate companies, which may be a big advantage if you work with a segment of real estate prices where commissions may represent a big percentage of the selling price. However, in order to sell your real estate directly, you will need a very solid platform, so that you do not miss good selling opportunities. Again, I point out to a website or a blog, and large social network accounts. In most countries, you can only promote your own homes and in some countries you may even need a real estate broker license to do that on a regular basis. Check the legislation in your own country.

3. ***Promote real estate in a very professional way***. One of the main ways to promote your real estate (if you decide to promote them yourself) if to have professional photographs. In order to do this, you need to consider hiring a photographer as you go or higher one on a monthly basis. Note, however, that if you hire a real estate company to promote your real estate, then it is possible that only they can promote it (always check for exclusivity agreements upfront).

4. **Do "open houses"**. Doing open houses is a great way to promote your real estate. Send an open letter and invite prospective buyers to join (again, check for possible conflicts in contracts with real estate agencies). Now you realize why promoting channels are so important, right?

10

Scale your portfolio until the million

To make a business out of your portfolio, you will need to scale it – until dozens of units, most likely. Of course this will depend on many variables, such as the type of properties you acquire, the market(s) you operate in, etc. For example, if you focus on small units, like shoebox condos in small markets, you will need a lot more units than if you focus on family homes in big markets (assuming some proportionality between rents and the sizes of homes and markets).

There are various variables that you must consider when growing a portfolio, because with growing a portfolio comes with a lot of pains and aches. In this chapter, I cover some of the solutions that can be used to overcome some of those difficulties. In particular, I will provide you with a recipe that I used when growing my own portfolio, and I observed in many large-scale investors, which is also part of the techniques that we use at my company, ArrowPlus.

Think big

There is no other way to go about it – to scale a portfolio, you must think big. Growing a portfolio is already hard enough, but it will be even harder if you do not have a vision (see Chapter 2) which includes a big portfolio. The chances of building a big portfolio starting with a small investment property and not seeing the plan beyond that, are very small. It is like trying to make an omelet without any eggs.

When planning a big portfolio, there are several different aspects that differ from smaller investments which I talked about until this chapter. Those aspects must be considered, and in this chapter I will talk about the most important aspects in this context. They include:

1. ***Logistics***. Creating a big portfolio requires specific logistics, which I will show you next.
2. ***Structure***. A big portfolio has to be looked at as a business, and as any business, it will require a structure. I will show you that a real estate business is a very unique one.
3. ***Type of entity***. I have talked about some financial differences between investing as an individual and as a company (see Chapter 5), however in this chapter I will explore this subject further, in the context of big portfolios.
4. ***Financing***. Although I have already covered this angle as well, big portfolios have very special financing conditions, which I will cover in this chapter.

Logistic aspects (and diversification)

Any big, well-structured portfolio requires efficient logistics to operate, otherwise there is the risk of failure. A big portfolio is way more susceptible to failure than small portfolios. The logistics of a big portfolio include visiting the properties, permanent contact with tenants, effective and cost-efficient maintenance, promoting the units, etc.

Many logistic services can be delegated to real estate companies, however it is likely that, for a sufficiently large portfolio, this will become a large cost and it is likely more profitable to hire one or more people to cover the logistics of the company/portfolio. Next, I will show you several examples of the logistics of large real estate portfolios.

Promoting properties is done through an own website and social network accounts, as I said before. However, you should realized that prospective clients (tenants or buyers) will not find these places by chance. In many cases, it is necessary to promote the channels themselves, for example with ads on socia networks and search engines. Additionally, managing these channels may require a lot of time, which should also be taken into account. Note that is is likely that you will get several requests to visit the properties, information requests, etc. In this category, it is also inserted the relationship with clients (including tenants) which is, in my opinion, a critical point of any business, and therefore where more resources should be deployed.

Probably, one of the most important aspects when considering the logistics of the company is visiting the properties, either to rent out or to sell. It is expected that you have several requests for visits, and although you can delegate these services to a real estate company, it is likely that we are talking about a higher cost than desired. To avoid that, you should consider employing at least one person (who may also take care of property promotion, if your portfolio is not too large yet). At the same time, you should consider that there is a cost to actually going to the properties, to show them.

Maintenance is another, real problem. Although you can hire companies to take care of maintenance, it is possible that that will cost too much money for a large portfolio. What I observed in large-scale portfolios is that they always have their own people to take care of maintenance, which is often taken care by someone who also takes care of promoting properties, visits them with prospective clients, and takes care of communication with tenants (remember the concept of a super?).

Lastly, I should tell you that diversification – usually regarded as a way to dilute risk – increases that problem. That is, if one hand it would be better (at least in theory) to invest in several real estate markets to avoid excessive exposure to a single market, on the other hand that will increase logistic costs, because distances to properties increase and perhaps more people needs to be hired. It is possible, however, to ensure logistics in a given city with the company's own resources and, while the volume in other cities is not big enough, hire other companies to do the job.

"Structure" or team

A bigger portfolio comes with more responsibilities, and it has more requirements than a smaller one. The truth is that the biggest advantage to a large portfolio is that, on average, you attain better results as you grow it. That is expected because investors tend to do better and better deals as they become more and more experienced. However, the requirements of a large portfolio, in terms of "structure", is way bigger than that of a small portfolio.

For instance, the probability of having to fight a lawsuit is generally bigger for bigger portfolios, and it is therefore recommended that you have a lawyer hired on a monthly basis. In fact, many lawyers will be receptive to work with you on a monthly value, and that will easily make sense once your portfolio grows beyond a specific point. Before that, you can simply hire a lawyer as you go, and chances are that your rental income is not enough to hire a lawyer permanently. At the same time, keep in mind that a lawyer may play a very important role in structuring a portfolio, as well as in creating, maintaining and expanding it.

Other examples of monthly services big portfolios require include photo services, to photograph your properties when promoting them and tax consultancy services, among others.

Financial aspects

It is complicated to determine how much a company has to make every year so that it can pay you a salary and have enough working capital. In other words, how much a company would have to make to survive. This also depends a lot on the country you live in, as taxes, write-offs, social security co-payments, and a myriad of other country-specific factors all come into play. Also, the type of company we are talking about makes a huge difference. For instance, a service-based company – meaning that there is no basis cost on the product to sell, other than the time spent by the employees and residual materials to accomplish that service – will have a very different business model than a company that buys and sells products.

For instance, imagine you own a service company that has no other employees other than yourself (let us assume residual costs as well). In this scenario, if you make $50.000, you will be able to pay for the operating costs of the company and still get a, say $30.000/yr salary. However, if your business model is based on selling one product (let us assume it costs you $100 and you sell it for $200) and your time is invested in selling that product, then you will have to generate $50.000 selling the products (with a $100 gross margin, you will need to sell 500 units). However, selling 500 units will get you to an yearly revenue of $100.000, twice as much as you would have to make in the service-based company so that you would end up with the same profit.

A real estate company also works with margins, and it is identical – from a business model standpoint - to a "buy and hold" portfolio at the individual level. In most countries, the main difference lies on taxes (personal vs corporate taxes) and the operational costs of the company. The gross margin of a company like this is the difference between the rental income and the costs incurred to obtain that income (maintenance, other costs with rental properties, interest on debt, etc).

Like I have written before, it is difficult to determine what is the minimum figure one has to make so that it makes sense to open a company. However, the examples above should provide you with a good idea of what to look for, when considering this question for your specific case.

Keep in mind that these examples are meant to give you just that – an idea. I recommend you talk to a licensed accountant about this subject, in order to accurately estimate after what point it pays off to set up a company to hold your real estate portfolio. However, if you plan on building a large portfolio, then it will probably be inevitable to set up a company at some point in time, due to the financial and the tax aspects, as well as the legal and the operation aspects.

Additional financing

In general, companies have better financing opportunities than individuals, especially if they hold large real estate portfolios. As in everything in this book, please note that your country may differ a lot from other countries, and nothing should be taken as a undisputed truth.

However, companies should present – just like individuals – solid histories and a perspective of stable income for the future. Many investors wonder whether they have better tax conditions if they buy real estate through a company, instead of doing it as individuals. Although it usually makes sense to invest in real estate through a corporation, there are many cases where it is not. For instance, I remember one client who asked me whether it made sense to invest in real estate through a company he already owned, and it clearly did not make any sense in his particular situation; his company had had no profit in the previous years, which prevented it from being financed. Banks and lenders will always assess the history of the companies with the banks, the financial history, and the perspective of future income. Thus, financing is a very important topic when planning to build a big portfolio through a company.

However, financing big portfolios goes well beyond banks and typical lenders. It is possible to invest together with business partners in some deals (where your company invests with some other entity – person or company - in a real estate deal), but it is also possible to include business partners in your company, becoming shareholders of the company. This is in fact a very important point when building a company to invest in real estate, because potential shareholders will assess the profits of the company, as well as dividend distributions. Therefore, if your goal is to grow the company to the point of financing it by selling stock to new shareholders, then you should structure the company since the beginning so that dividend distribution is optimized.

Lastly, another example of exterior financing is to get loans from other entities than banks and typical lenders. Currently, there are some companies and individuals that lend money to businesses, which is also a possibility for real estate investment companies. Either way, it is necessary to plan for optimal dividend payment history and debt payment history, as those are the angles that most investors will value the most.

Sell yourself to an investor

Do you realize now why your portfolio's history should be very attractive, among other things, as far as dividend distribution and debt payback history? Here is the cold reality: most people will have to go after investors, not the other way around. And as any business contact, you will have to be able to sell your product well – in this case your portfolio's performance.

As a portfolio investor, I would try to quickly determine how fast I would get my money back (expecting it to be 4 years or less, in this particular investment), and what would be the quality of the portfolio I would be investing in, both in terms of properties and markets. In other words, I would like to recoup my money as soon as possible and invest in the best possible markets and assets. In my opinion, a good market is one that has a good offer/demand ratio, as well as good sustainability and appreciation.

Therefore, you can sell yourself to an investor by showing that your portfolio has a phenomenal performance history and a good future perspective, by having solid assets, in good markets. Of course that you will have to be 100% transparent with every possible investor. My belief is that you should plan to had foreign investors coming in since day 1, if that is your intention. You should thoughrouly control dividend payouts and buy good, solid assets that are suitable for the quality you want for your portfolio.

The millionaire portfolio

Becoming a millionaire through real estate is one of the most known and tested ways to accumulate wealth. Real estate as many advantages over other investment vehicles, and if your goal is to become a millionaire, then it is even more obvious the advantage of real estate, as I show you in this chapter.

My experience tells me that, if we take the factors I mentioned in this chapter into account, then building a millionaire portfolio has the very same basis, whether the investor wants to attain one or several millions. Over the years, by contacting with many real estate investors and by building my own portfolio, I realized that it is possible to divide the goal to attain the millionaire portfolio into 3 different phases, as I show you next.

Step 1: think like a millionaire

Do you remember what I told you in Chapter 2 about having a vision? And what I told you in this chapter about thinking big? I cannot stress this point enough: thinking big, like a millionaire, is the only real chance of becoming successful in the creation of a millionaire portfolio. Do not believe that big projects where accomplished by chance or without an initial, almost stubborn vision. For instance, would you believe if someone told you that huge portfolios were built by chance? Or that huge companies like Apple or Tesla were formed without a big, solid vision behind them? Confidence, belief and determination are absolutely necessary in every idea. And with that, I want to tell you that it is not enough to desire and envision having a millionaire portfolio: you have to act from day 1 like so.

One of the most frequent problems I see, especially among investors in my country, is "stepping over dollars to save pennies". If you analyze how millionaires structure their investments and how they allocate their time and money, you will realize that, often, they "macro-manage" these things. It makes sense that small investors who are taking the first steps in real estate investing, invest their time "micro-managing" some aspects of their financial life, saving wherever they can. For instance, I accept the fact that a beginner investor spends an entire morning of his week comparing prices of materials needed for his first renovation.

However, this is not what a big investor would do. I believe that big investors would rather allocate their time on other things, such as planning their portfolio as a whole, looking for the next great deal, etc. It all comes down to how we value our time and the yield we get out of it. For instance, I do not see myself spending an entire morning to save 100 buck on a new appliance. To me, one morning is worth a lot more than that.

The second aspect is planning. You should plan for a portfolio and a structure truly scalable, from day 1, that does not have any growth limitation.

There are several examples of non-scalable portfolios. Imagine a portfolio that is centered on great opportunities rather than great markets. Investing in great opportunities may mean investing in a very diversified way, in many markets, thus increasing the number of commissions (to sell and rent out) and maintenance, over time, as I said before. If you would invest in a given market – a market that is generally good vs a single deal that is awesome – you will, in principle, make more investments in that market, does making sense to set up a logistic structure (e.g. a team to take care of maintenance and promoting your properties) at some point.

In a large portfolio, this could make a huge difference. Therefore, I always recommend investors to carefully plan their portfolios carefully. Many investors do that naturally. Others look for help to do that. My company provides market studies to help investors structure their portfolios, so they become more scalable. I usually recommend investors to find a consultancy company that does affordable market studies on real estate to plan their portfolio, so they do it based on solid data.

Finally, millionaire investors also possess another quality: they really do not care about the generalized beliefs about some investments, markets, products, etc – they typically want to find out about those themselves. Big investors are "the few who can recognize a lot of value in places and opportunities where many find little to no value". For instance, many investors made fortunes trading and speculating on commodities, especially the cheapest ones – where little saw any value. Smaller markets in real estate can be an interesting option, even if they are not regarded as so. The best opportunities are sometimes in properties (and types of properties) that no one sees value in. Let your gut guide you, based on solid data, but free from pre-defined concepts.

Step 2: buy a million

Although this may look very difficult, it may be easier than you think. Buying a million dollars or euros in real estate is not the same it was back then. In fact, if you consider you "only" have to have 20% to put down on a real estate property or a set of properties, then you will buy a million in real estate with "only" $200.000. It just got simpler, right?

To buy a million dollars or euros in real estate – if your goal is to set up a millionaire portfolio – you should look for properties whose cost/worth is as low as possible, which will accelerate the goal and allow you to leverage (i.e. finance your deals) in an easier way. However, you should note that this does not mean that these properties are necessarily those that offer the highest yields. For instance, it is possible that the yield of a property bought for $200.000 and appraised at $200.000 is higher than another property also bought for $200.000 but appraised at $400.000. Again, I stress that if the main goal is to attain a millionaire portfolio as fast as possible, then this could be an important strategy.

As I said before, financing can be a fundamental piece of the puzzle, when it comes to buying a million bucks in real estate. Financing through banks is perhaps the easiest, quickest and more standard, but other sources, such as angel investors, business partners and others can be important alternatives, as I have mentioned before.

Note that, as I said before, it is easier to increase your wealth if you are already (at least moderately) wealthy. First, you can finance yourself using your wealth, thus leveraging on it. Secondly, you will be more creditworthy before a financier if you are already wealthy (or have some wealth/real estate, for that matter). History will matter a lot too. Banks will also look a lot to credit history, as I said before. While a history with a bank will matter a lot, a history of businesses can make you go farther with investors – they will always want to see your records and history of previously made deals. One important thing is to show that you can leverage on the income of previously bought properties to grow the profits of the portfolio (for instance, by buying more properties).

With this data and a solid plan, both regarding buying good properties/assets and following a financial plan, it is possible to buy your first million in real estate.

Step 3: own a million

Once you have bought a million bucks in real estate, you now must own that million to be considered a millionaire. In step 2 you already had, legally speaking, a millionaire portfolio. However, you had debt on it, meaning that you did not have a million dollars in net worth.

In this step, the goal is either to pay off enough debt so that your net worth hits one million or continue to increase your portfolio (perhaps by creating more debt) so that your net worth (i.e. the difference between the assets and the debt) becomes a million bucks. This last perspective is widely used in countries like the US, where investors think about their positions in real estate as "equity". In Europe, this is usually not the case, as investors tend to look at their positions in real estate as binary (either they own it free and clear or they do not). Europe is a large continent with many different countries, and I am not insinuating all countries share the same real estate cultures, so in your country this may not be the case, fellow European!

The equity perspective is simple: if you paid 25% of your home and it is worth $200.000, then you own $50.000 worth of equity in that home, regardless how much you owe the bank/lender (in this case $150.000 plus interest). If you do not possess more assets, then your entire net worth is also $50.000.

In the first "model", which focuses on paying off as much as debt as quickly as possible, in order to achieve a million in equity, the focus is usually to use the rental income to pay off debt as much and as quickly as possible. In this model, it is also normal to negotiate prepayment penalties, so that lenders waive them. On a normal mortgage, prepayment penalties are different depending whether you have a fixed or an adjustable interest rate. You should pay close attention to these penalties and negotiate them, if you can, if you go with this model.

In the second model, where you leverage as much as possible based on your portfolio (in principle it will be easier to be financed as your portfolio grows), there are a few things to talk about. First, you should thoroughly control the ratio between debt and assets' worth. As you increase debt, you should make sure that your assets worth increases (at least, linearly) with the debt.

However, in this model, you are more exposed to the future value of your assets, because they can appreciate less than you can expect. In particular, if they depreciate or appreciate less than you expect, they may not even be enough to cover all the debt you create. If you follow this model, then the main focus should continue to be acquiring high-yield properties, in the chosen markets. That is, even if you can buy assets with excellent appraisals/acquisition cost ratios, it does not mean that such properties are the best ones to go with, if the yields of the properties are not attractive. In a nutshell, the sustainability of this model is ensured through a carefull selection of properties to acquire. At the same time, in this model, you should pay attention to over- or fast-growth, which increases the risk involved. In theory, the risk of this model is much higher than in the previous model.

11

Keep yourself at the top

Once you have built a portfolio you are happy with – regardless we are talking about a million-dollars portfolio or not – the next step should be to "keep yourself at the top". That is, keeping yourself in a comfortable position regarding your goals, holding on to that position. A big portfolio (or a mid-sized one, for that matter) comes with a lot of responsibility and a bigger structure. Therefore, the investor is more susceptible to make mistakes. Think about a one- or two-property portfolio, compared to one that is composed of a dozen or even hundreds of homes. Of course that the second scenario is way more error-prone, and there is a higher likelihood of incurring problems and headaches.

Over time, I have identified a set of aspects that I consider paramount to maintain a decent-sized portfolio. When I say "maintain", I do not mean "maintenance", but instead maintain the portfolio itself, and is structure, so that you maintain your business in the most protected and profitable way possible.

Protection

Protection is probably the most important aspect of maintaining a large portfolio. Although the frequency at which tenants sue landlords varies a lot from country to country, there is always the inherent risk that you, as a landlord, get sued. There are a myriad of reasons why landlords can be sued, and therefore I cannot list them all here. However, there are common situations why this happens, which an attorney can easily and quickly tell you. My advice is to hire an attorney in your country, in particular one who is specialized in real estate, in order to determine exactly the best way to legally structure your portfolio and protect yourself (insurance is a big part of this and comes later in this book).

Legal counseling

As I said before, you should have a permanent attorney to provide you legal counseling. If you already have a large portfolio, you know that you will need to question an attorney is fairly high (thus, a monthly agreement will probably be more beneficial). You should also have a meeting with your attorney to decide what terms should you act under, and what angles of your business you should protect and how. A very important thing to do is to choose an attorney who specializes in real estate and has more clients who have real estate investing portfolios. Otherwise, it will be difficult for an attorney to answer all questions that pop up when managing a large real estate portfolio, or at least it will be harder for him/her than for another attorney who specializes in real estate and has experience in the industry.

At the same time, choose someone who can work well with email; from my experience, there will be a ton of problems if you decide to work with someone who does not recognize email as a basic communication tool; plus, you want to have all information written down, to avoid misunderstandings, and to forward that information to other people such as e.g. tenants, if necessary. Plus, I recommended to talk to tenants over email as well, so it would just be easier to cc your attorney if need be (which is only possible if he/she works with email).

A very important point regarding the legal aspect of your portfolio is to determine the legal form of your investment entity, something that should be done earlier in the game. The legal form of the entity you set up to invest can make a lot of difference when dealing with legal and fiscal processes. As I said before, it is possible that you make your investments as an individual (and therefore not needing to set up another entity), but you should to discuss that with your legal counselor. Although many investors prefer to have their portfolios as individuals, it is important to understand the consequences of that.

This will depend a lot on your country's law and general legislation, but usually a few properties are needed in order to outweigh the costs of setting up a company. Setting up a company involves some costs, which I have already talked about (cf. Chapter 5). However, it is crucial to understand the differences between investing at the personal level and from a company, something you should discuss with your legal counselor (and with your tax advisor, as taxes are a big component of the answer to this question).

Moreover, you should keep your legal counselor informed of every step you take while building your portfolio. The most obvious point is to keep your legal counselor informed of every leasing contract you celebrate with your tenants, while letting him know of all important communication with tenants and other entities. However, there are many other steps you should keep your legal counselor informed about. For instance, have him know about all contracts that pertain to renovation works, financing, etc. Always ask for his/her opinion and have him/her review the steps you take. This will save you a lot of time, money and worries down the line.

Insurance

Sadly, there are many properties that are not insured even for the minimum required by each country's law (for instance, insurance to cover a fire in the property). I always recommend investors to be as insured and protected as possible, anticipating the scenarios that can happen with his/her properties and what responsibility they entail. For instance, I always recommend investors to get the most wide insurance possible, for each property bought, and have a social liability insurance, which covers potential damage to others and others' assets through their real estate properties. Also, pay attention to any co-payments (also called excess) – i.e. the amount of money you have to pay on each claim - of different insurance.

Do not let yourself believe that "bad things only happen to other people", thus trying to save on insurance cost to increase the profit of your real estate investments. Do it the other way around: consider adequate protection to your properties before you buy them, and do the math of the investment factoring in the cost of that protection.

Bigger portfolios, especially those that are built through companies, should have even broader insurance, compared to real estate properties that are owned as an individual. Set up a formal meeting with an insurance broker you rely on and try to figure out, together with him, what are the best ways to insure your portfolio and limit your responsibility; "keep yourself at the top" is all about playing safe.

Although I stress that you should schedule a meeting with an insurance broker who you rely on (or you have great references of, should you know no broker), I will leave you some points that should be useful:

1. Insure damage on the properties but also damage caused by you property on other people, and your own social liability. Consider having a social liability insurance for yourself and one for the company you invest through, should that be the scenario.

2. Always insure your furniture and other content in your properties, including structural furniture (e.g. kitchen cabinets), in the widest array of scenarios. This is typically done with contents insurance. Usually, in similar insurances, the assets/contents of tenants are not included – either way let them know, so there are no misunderstandings (and give them the chance to insure their own assets).

3. Pay close attention to co-payments and excess figures, i.e. how much money you will have to pay in every claim. Although co-payments usually make insurance way cheaper, most of the time, from my experience there are co-payments that are simply too high. In order to cover yourself on a very wide way, choose insurance without co-payments. Talk to your insurance broker about this and have him advise you on the best insurances.

4. Pay attention to all aspects of the insurance policies you are offered. For instance, some insurances do not cover esthetic damage. That means that, if you claim damage due to e.g. a broken pipe in the bathroom, the insurance may cover the replacement of the pipes themselves, and new tiles, but only in the area where the damage happened, thus ensuring that the bathroom stays functional. However, in this case the new tile used in the damaged area will be different from the rest of the tile in the bathroom (and you would have to pay for the rest of the tile if you wanted to look all the same). Talk to your insurance broker about fine details like this, before contained in policies.

Bulletproof business models

So far, I provided with you generic recommendations for any portfolio. They do not depend on a given business model, strategy or approach to real estate investing.

However, there are several aspects that can be integrated in real estate business models, in order to increase the resilience of those portfolios, especially in what pertains to inflation, the economy's performance, trends, etc. There are some of those aspects:

1. *Think "safe"*. As I said before, there are specific real estate deals that are based on specific premises when they are closed. For instance, if you acquire a property close to a university – to rent out to students – you are probably assuming that the university will not close in the following years. Universities and colleges do have an advantage over other types of entities: in the short term, they are not expected to close their doors. Although that is not impossible, the truth is that Ivy League universities that have been around for a long time are not expected to close, in a short time-frame, with high likelihood.

2. *Index your rental income to inflation*. If one of your tenants asks a bank for a loan, he/she will not find it odd to have an adjustable rate. However, if you as a landlord try to use an index in the rent, making it adjustable, tenants will dispute that right away...

There are, however, legal ways to increase rents according to inflation or similar indexes. Many countries' rental laws specify specific legal coefficients that can be used to automatically increase rents. However, according to some legislations, you will need to specify in the leasing contract that you are allowed, as a landlord, to use this index and update the rent every year. This is a very important thing to do, because otherwise you may be stuck with a very low rent for a long time (if there are no rent updates, tenants will try to lock the contract for a long time, which can then become a financial burden in countries with tenant-friendly laws). Also, note that these compound as well; if 1% or even 2% per year may sound like peanuts, it will compound nicely over say a 10% period. Talk to an attorney about this subject and have him prepare a contract that factors this problem in.

3. *Diversify, even to "peculiar" markets, if need be*. Diversification is typically used to dilute risk in real estate portfolios and investments in general. Therefore, to increase the resilience of your portfolio, you should regard diversification as something always inevitable. Remember what I told you in Chapter 10, about the logistic aspects of diversification.

Diversifying does not imply investing in faraway markets or even new markets. You can choose to diversify to near markets. But you can also diversify the kind of investments you make in one given market. For instance, the type of property you buy, whether you address residential or commercial real estate, or the entity they depend on the most (e.g. rentals close to colleges to rent out to students, units close to hospitals to rent out to nurses and physicians, etc).

But you can go further in this regard. Today, tourism is growing fast within Europe and there is now an entire new market based on AirBnBs and short-term rentals. This market is considerably different from the classic rental market, and even though it has comes with higher and more complex logistics, it is generally more profitable yield-wise. As I said before, this is in fact vertical to every kind of investment, as there is usually a trade-off between the yield and how passive the investment is. Short-term rentals to tourists generally offer higher yields, at the cost of higher logistics.

4. *Always keep your team posted*. Regarding your legal counseling, as I said before, you should always keep your attorney posted about the decisions you take, especially those that impact your portfolio and your plan. However, you should go way beyond that: keep the rest of your team members (maintenance guys, people who interact with tenants, etc) posted all the time, and make sure the team can execute properly. For instance, ask your tenants to communicate problems to an e-mail list where all maintenance and communication people are. Make sure there are no flaws at that level: communication with tenants has to be professional and efficient; This will lower early lease terminations and vacancies while increase the average duration of your leases and the overall performance of the portfolio.

5. *Have backups*. I always recommend investors that pay me for consultancy work to have backups in their portfolios. By backups I mean reserves. Financial reserves that anticipate worse times (from long vacancies to lawsuits or even unexpected – and expensive - maintenance in your properties). As they say, hope for the best, plan for the worst. The simple rule I suggest investors is to have a financial backup/fund of 6-12 month portfolio expenses (taxes, insurance, maintenance - I typically estimate 1-2% of each property value - etc). This should also include mortgage installments, if you do have debt, and vacancies (although a conservative vacancy expectation will do, often). A simple alternative to this is to follow the 1% rule, which I presented in Chapter 5 as the security/emergency fund. Bad times may be a reality, and a financial reserve is definitely a crucial part of any "bulletproof" portfolio.

Artur Mariano

12

After this book

Real estate investing is a complex game, with many peculiar aspects. I introduced you several of those aspects in this book, based on years of my own experience. Let us be realistic: if you read this book and you do not apply what you learned, you will not gain anything from it. I believe that investing in real estate is one of the best paths to create and increase wealth, due to the various reasons I presented in this book. I also believe that, when executed based on solid knowledge, and calculated risk, it can be an excellent investment. However, as with everything in life, it will take your best effort and dedication in order for you to become successful.

There is a set of final things I would like to cover in this chapter – things that you should take into account when starting your investments or take them to the next level. You can do it based on what you learn on this book about real estate investment, but you should keep in mind that no measure is universal, which is to say that no true is absolute. And always remember: in theory, practice is equal to theory, but in practice it is not!

Put into practice

As any investment, real estate has some risk associated. It is up to each investor to obtain the maximum information possible, about the sector and the investments he/she chooses to invest in, so that the investment is made based on a calculated risk. At the same time, obtaining too much information will not take you further. That is, you may know all about a specific industry – such as real estate – but knowledge is not enough; putting things into practice is absolutely necessary, but it is something a lot of people have problems with. As time went by, I was able to observe a very large number of people who acquired a vast knowledge about real estate investing but never invested a single dollar into it. Even though I understand that this can be daunting and intimidating task for a lot of people, it is equally true that one tree only grows if it is planted and watered. It is often necessary to break the natural human resistance to avoid risk and failure.

When starting to invest, you should be as careful as possible. Consider the points I presented you in this book about e.g. protection and financial reserves (Chapters 5 and 12), and that investing is an essential instrument in the current economy, but it must be understood and you should consult a licensed advisor who you trust in. When putting your knowledge into practice, you should pay attention to the aspects I present next.

The best for your own case

Mas task in this book is to convey you the best possible information, introducing you to real estate investment models and strategies. However, there is no perfect model or strategy, especially at a global scale (otherwise all investors would apply the same model and be successful). In fact, there is a simple proof to this: real estate investing books all present different angles and opinions. What is the best path for me may not be the best path to you, and the other way around. Each investor has a different risk profile, which is probably more suitable for a specific strategy. I gave you information; it is now up to you to determine what is best for your own case.

Thus, I invite you to assess everything that I brought you, in terms of knowledge, with this book, especially what pertains to:

1. Strategy. As I showed you in Chapter 3, there are known, tested strategies and models to invest in real estate. You will have to choose, based on your profile, taste and knowledge, what is the best plan to follow. Personally, I prefer the buy and hold strategy, however each investor has a specific profile, with specific goals, and those will determine the best strategy. It is, however, very important to keep in mind that the strategy you choose will determine the set of actions to take.

2. *Capital to invest*. Although real estate is a tested form, over time, to increase individual wealth, I do not want to convey the idea that you should invest all your capital, let alone investing at all. You should always consider that there are many setbacks and unpredicted situations in life, such as sickness. Common sense should still come first, and only you will know what part of your net worth you can and you are willing to invest into real estate. Be reasonable and consult a licensed advisor before investing, so that you can structure your savings and investments, if you can do it and you feel it is necessary.

3. *Risk- and debt-tolerance*. As you can imagine, I have been able to observe over time, different types of clients, with all kinds of risk and debt tolerances. Debt is especially important in this context because it generally increases the risk of an investment. Although I had clients that were very inclined towards risk deals, the majority of investors (especially those who are starting out) have low tolerance to risk. Regardless the rest, define your own tolerance levels to risk. Understand whether it makes sense to get into debt to invest – and do it together with someone experienced and preferably a financial advisor that you trust in, or a company that has a solid history in the industry.

4. *Time to dedicate*. The last vector of this subject, for any real estate investor who is starting out, is the time to dedicate to those investments. This is actually, in my opinion, one of the biggest mistakes of many investors who are taking the first steps into real estate investing: they do not calculate the time they need to dedicate to their investments correctly.

Although ArrowPlus offers passive real estate investments in Portugal, that is usually not the general rule for investments in general: the majority of investors usually decide to manage their own investments, which entails communication with tenants, thus requiring a lot of time and dedication from you. You will need to determine whether you have that extra time to invest towards the management of your real estate portfolio.

Keep doing what worked for you

Perhaps you are already a successful real estate investor, and you wanted to read this book because you know my work or you simply want to know (even) more about this industry. However, although I expect this book has opened your horizons to real estate investing, that does not necessarily mean that you should rethink what you have done up until know – in particular, if you have had success! In other words, if what you have done so far worked for you, even if it is different from what I presented you, you should keep doing what you have done so far. I hope, though, that this book brought you a new, more solid structure in terms of knowledge and tools, and allow you to have another look at what you have done and can improve.

Over time, we make our own path, with a singular way of thinking and acting. Several different paths can have similar success, though. What really matters is to act based on solid knowledge and experience, regardless of its origin, shape and form. If you have developed a strategy of your own, that is totally different from what I suggest in this book, do not find it odd. And do not change anything just because this book says so – do it at your own risk, but above all, do it based on your intuition regarding the information I presented you.

Knowledge does not end here

You may have read this book and now you think you know all about real estate investing. Although I believe that this book conveys very solid knowledge on real estate investing, and it will be a great return on your time and money, I do not think that knowledge ends with it.

First of all, if you liked this book, I invite you to follow my work, and check real estate investing courses that I am currently working on. There are simply too many aspects of real estate investing, and some of them I could not cover in this book due to being too specific, complex, long or simply not blending well with the rest of this book.

Secondly, keep in mind that practice is the best way to learn about anything. Although real estate investing implies a cost per se, which you cannot reverse easily if you make a mistake, there are several intermediate processes that are free and will allow you to start acquiring experience in the area. For instance, searching for real estate properties on the ground, talking with real estate agents and other investors, and doing your research on real estate prices and rents, are some of the steps you can take without incurring any costs, at the same time you start gaining experience. Plus, if you plan on remodeling properties as part of your plan, then you can start with the tips I gave you on having good relationships with retail store managers, developers/contractors, etc.

Final words

It is my deepest desire that you have success in your real estate investments. It is also my belief that this book will be of great help in your path, but it is above all it is your responsibility to put all the knowledge you have gotten into practice.

Writing about investment can sometimes be difficult, because the author can give the readers some directions, in a naïve way, and then look responsible for any consequence of that investment. I would like to stress that, as the author of this book, I am by no means responsible for your investments (check the disclaimer in the beginning of the book), but even then I always recommend investors a gradual investment policy, controlled and based on the available capital of each investor. As everything in life, be responsible and use common sense, knowing your limits and never crossing them.

I also want to tell you that the best investments in life are those that make us happy. I have a particular taste for real estate, since a young age, and I let that taste come through in the properties I renovate. And that is only because I love what I do – and I feel I contribute to creating value and improve the landscape of the cities I invest in. At the end of the day, that is what matters in life: you may look at investment anywhere from a side-hustle to a full-time passion. Even if you do it for the financial factor (there is no problem with that, like I said before), have pleasure with what you do – even in the smallest things.

As I final recommendation, which is something vertical to all aspects of life, I want to tell you that in every of your actions – regarding investments or not – do good, be fair and generous, and always be kind with others – I deeply believe that the universe will give back to you in an unbelievable way.

www.ingramcontent.com/pod-product-compliance
Lightning Source LLC
Chambersburg PA
CBHW030655220526
45463CB00005B/1787